I'll SAY YES

and trust God with the rest

AMBER OLAFSSON

I'll Say Yes—Copyright ©2022 by Amber Olafsson

Published by UNITED HOUSE Publishing

All rights reserved. No portion of this book may be reproduced or shared in any form—electronic, printed, photocopied, recording, or by any information storage and retrieval system, without prior written permission from the publisher. The use of short quotations is permitted.

Unless otherwise indicated, all Scripture quotations are taken from the Holy Bible, New Living Translation, copyright © 1996, 2004, 2015 by Tyndale House Foundation. Used by permission of Tyndale House Publishers, Carol Stream, Illinois 60188. All rights reserved.

Scripture quotations marked (NIV) are taken from the Holy Bible, New International Version®, NIV®. Copyright © 1973, 1978, 1984, 2011 by Biblica, Inc.™ Used by permission of Zondervan. All rights reserved worldwide. www.zondervan.com The "NIV" and "New International Version" are trademarks registered in the United States Patent and Trademark Office by Biblica, Inc.™

Scripture marked (KJV) are taken from The Authorized (King James) Version. Rights in the Authorized Version in the United Kingdom are vested in the Crown. Reproduced by permission of the Crown's patentee, Cambridge University Press

Scripture taken from the New King James Version®. Copyright © 1982 by Thomas Nelson. Used by permission. All rights reserved.

Scripture taken from The Voice™. Copyright © 2012 by Ecclesia Bible Society. Used by permission. All rights reserved.

The Holy Bible, Berean Standard Bible, BSB Copyright ©2016, 2020 by Bible Hub Used by Permission. All Rights Reserved Worldwide.

ISBN: 978-1-952840-26-5

UNITED HOUSE Publishing

Clarkston, Michigan
info@unitedhousepublishing.com
www.unitedhousepublishing.com

Cover and interior design: Amber Olafsson
Cover and interior layout: Matt Russell, mrussell@marketing-image.com
Front, back cover, and author bio photography: Drew Olafsson

Printed in the United States of America
2022—First Edition

SPECIAL SALES
Most UNITED HOUSE books are available at special quantity discounts when purchased in bulk by corporations, organizations, and special-interest groups. For information, please e-mail orders@unitedhousepublishing.com

*To my husband and best friend, Andrew.
Thank you for walking with me through every YES
I've given to God. Living this adventurous life
with you is the only way I would have it!*

CONTENTS

Introduction 7
Being Available 10
1 - I lose a friend 17
2 - I'm scared 25
3 - I might get punched 35
4 - I want to say no 43
Living Interrupted 54
5 - I don't want to 59
6 - I feel unqualified 71
7 - I don't know how 81
8 - It's not in my plan 97
9 - I don't think I'm the one for the job 109
Starting Small 120
10 - I have no training for this 125
11 - I do not have the money 137
12 - I don't like it 151
13 - I'm not a pastor 163
14 - I don't how it's going to work out 177
15 - It's not what I expected 185
Willing Vessels 196
16 - I get called crazy 201
Conclusion 223
Your Yes Story 225
Say yes to a Relationship with Jesus 226
Say Yes to the Holy Spirit 228
Acknowledgements 231
Bibliography 237
About the Author 239

INTRODUCTION

When I reach the end of my life, I don't want to look back and wonder what might have happened if I would have said YES. Say yes to what? Stay tuned, you are about to find out!

If you're looking for advice on how to live a comfortable, predictable, and "normal" life, then you've picked up the wrong book. You see, I gave up routines, control, and living in my comfort zone a long time ago. I think normal is overrated anyway. But if you're looking to live a life of adventure with the Lord, then you're in the right place.

In case you haven't been informed, I must tell you: God is unpredictable. My life took a drastic turn when I made a deal with Him. Yep, I did that. For context, you need to know I'm a church kid; I was there every time the doors were open. Sunday morning, Sunday night, and Wednesday night, for my entire life—but while I spent much of my time in His house, I didn't know His Spirit at all. I wanted this to change. I longed to discern the voice of the Holy Spirit more than anything, so if He instructed me to "Go!" I *would* recognize His call and *wouldn't* hesitate to drop everything and move. Do you long to hear His voice, too? They say if you want something you've never had, you've got to do something you've never done… so I leapt into the unknown.

What was the deal I struck with God? I made a bold declaration, "Alright Holy Spirit, if you ask me to do something, I'll say YES." This has been our agreement ever since. And guys, it is only one word, but trust me when I tell you those three letters, Y-E-S, are life-changing when offered to the Creator of the universe. This book is my journey from the distant land of stale religion into the glorious Kingdom of God at hand, one YES at a time.

Now, take a look at those chapter titles. You know what they represent? Excuses—reasons that often stop us from giving God our YES. I had them ALL, my friend. I hope as you witness how I overcame common objections, it will build courage and break down any obstacle holding you back.

As you read the stories of how an average person found the tenacity to leave her comfort zone and become bold, you might start believing God could use someone like you, too. Don't live in regret, wondering what may have been different if you had said YES to God; let my God-stories inspire a few of your own. Let's get this party started! 'Cause ain't no party like a Holy Ghost party 'cause a Holy Ghost party don't stop.

BEING AVAILABLE

FORGET. IT. That's what I need you to do. If you've been in church any amount of time, you have probably heard the parable of the talents. But I'm going to need you to pretend like you've never read it before. Imagine this is the first time you've seen this passage and let's see what God reveals.

"For the Kingdom of Heaven is just like a man about to go on a journey. He called his own servants and entrusted his possessions to them. To one he gave five talents, to another two talents, and to another one talent, depending on each one's ability. Then he went on a journey. Immediately the man who had received five talents went, put them to work, and earned five more. In the same way the man with two earned two more. But the man who had received one talent went off, dug a hole in the ground, and hid his master's money.

"After a long time the master of those servants came and settled accounts with them. The man who had received five talents approached, presented five more talents, and said, 'Master, you gave me five talents. See, I've earned five more talents.'

"His master said to him, 'Well done, good and faithful servant! You were faithful over a few things; I will put you in charge of many things. Share your master's joy.'

"The man with two talents also approached. He said, 'Master, you gave me two talents. See, I've earned two more talents.'

"His master said to him, 'Well done, good and faithful servant! You were faithful over a few things; I will put you in charge of many things. Share your master's joy.'

"The man who had received one talent also approached and said, 'Master, I know you. You're a harsh man, reaping where you haven't sown and gathering where you haven't scattered seed. So I was afraid and went off and

hid your talent in the ground. See, you have what is yours.'

"His master replied to him, 'You evil, lazy servant! If you knew that I reap where I haven't sown and gather where I haven't scattered, then you should have deposited my money with the bankers, and I would have received my money back with interest when I returned.

"'So take the talent from him and give it to the one who has ten talents. For to everyone who has, more will be given, and he will have more than enough. But from the one who does not have, even what he has will be taken away from him." Matthew 25:14-30

Let's cut right to the chase. What's up with this: *"So take the talent from him and give it to the one who has ten talents"*? Perhaps, like me, you may be particularly bothered by this sentence at first glance. When I voiced this to God, my conversation with Him didn't go at all like I thought it would.

What?! You took away the one talent from the "scared guy" and gave it to the one who has ten?! What's up with that God?! Rich boy already has plenty of money! Now, this ain't right!

God replied, "What if this isn't about money? What if those talents are opportunities?"

Wait, WHAT??????

Mind literally blown.

After I peeled my gaping mouth up off the floor, I read the passage one more time, and the whole story transformed. So, this isn't about God taking money from the poor and giving it to the rich because they didn't know how to invest it or removing gifts from those who don't use them and offering those to people who are more talented? Instead, this story offers us insight into how His Kingdom works, revealing that God is watching to see if we'll use the opportunities He gives us. It doesn't matter if it is ten, five, or one, every opportunity has the potential to turn into more opportunities.

In a split second, I saw why the master took the talent, or should I say "opportunity," and gave it to the one who had plenty. If we're not going to make the most of every chance God gives us, why would He offer us more? It makes complete sense that if we don't jump on the opportunity offered before us, walking through every door He opens, the Lord would move right along and give it to someone who will say YES. He's not looking for those who will waste opportunities, who won't walk through the doorway. He is looking for people who will seize every opportunity— whether they feel qualified or not, talented or not, wise or not, rich or not—and say YES to every door He opens. A person who will radically commit to saying YES to God is considered good and faithful. These are the ones He is looking for.

So take the talent from him and give it to the one who has ten talents. For to everyone who has, more will be given, and he will have more than enough. But from the one who does not have, even what he has will be taken away from him.

Once I understood what this story represented, something took root in my soul: I became determined to never let any opportunity be taken from me and given to another who

> **I BECAME DETERMINED TO NEVER LET ANY OPPORTUNITY BE TAKEN FROM ME AND GIVEN TO ANOTHER WHO WAS MORE WILLING.**

was more willing. I was not going to be "that guy." I decided, while I may not have the most ability, I would have the most availability—to God. I would say YES, no matter the cost... and it has a cost, but the reward has been a rich, fulfilling life packed with God adventures. So I ask: Are you willing to make yourself available for God?

1

I'LL SAY YES
Even if...
I lose a friend

I do not want to do this. I begrudgingly protested when I got my first opportunity to say YES to God. I knew it was the Holy Spirit, because the request came out of nowhere and I did not want to comply. What He asked of me was a good thing, but it was a hard thing. He never said it would be easy. In fact, if the opportunity presented is a difficult, uncomfortable request, it's likely God because we don't usually think up uncomfortable situations for ourselves. And if you are unsure if it is His voice, seek further wise counsel. Always be led in peace. You may be nervous, but if it is God, He will provide supernatural confidence in the midst of shaky nerves.

So, let me tell you about my first "opportunity." While dropping off a meal to a brand new mama, her demeanor communicated turmoil. She proceeded to tell me about her horrible hospital experience, and because of the excruciating pain, she could barely turn her head. I felt awful for her and wished I knew how to help. We had been friends for a while, she knew I went to church but I rarely talked about God. I remember thinking: *If this was one of my "church friends" I would offer to pray for her,* but I didn't want to be pushy, offend, or if I'm honest, risk losing a friend. It was at this moment the Holy Spirit whispered something to my heart.

"I want you to pray with her."

I was not comfortable with this, so of course, I resisted. *What? No! I can't do that. What if she gets mad at me and doesn't want to be my friend anymore?*

"You said you were going to say yes to the next thing I asked you to do."

I said I would try. Big emphasis on 'try.'

"Are you going to do this or not?"

Ok, fine. Yes, I'll do it, but I don't want to.

I wanted to hear the voice of the Holy Spirit more than anything, and if saying YES was the path to more of Him, I had to, even if it meant I lost a friend. So I relented. I stepped out of my circle of comfort and took a leap into the scary unknown. I was confident it was His voice, but I wasn't confident about what would happen.

Then, I nervously asked my friend if it would be okay if I prayed for her, and I braced for rejection… but it never came. Instead, she said yes! I couldn't believe it. Internally, my mouth was open wide in shock, externally, I kept my composure while I thought *Seriously? Dang, okay, God! You actually know what you are doing!* I proceeded to lay my hands on her shoulder and prayed for healing, peace, and for things to get better. And then, she started crying. She. Cried. Y'all.

What?? I was flabbergasted and in awe of what God was doing. Afterward, she thanked me for "caring enough to pray for her!!" This was a big deal for me. It marked the first time I intentionally left my comfort zone at the word of the Lord. Check out this secret I discovered in the parable of the talents which gave me the courage to step out:

For it is just like a man about to go on a journey. He called his own servants and entrusted his possessions to them. To one he gave five talents, to another two talents, and to another one talent, <u>depending on each one's ability</u>.

Did you notice the last word: ability? Well, that's a *special* word. This story unveiled something very integral for anyone committed to this "I'll Say Yes" journey: What God asks us to do, we will be *able*, but we may not be *comfortable*. For example, I am capable of praying for people. I pray with my Christian friends all the time. Offering up a prayer is totally within my ability. But where it crossed the comfort line was being asked to pray for someone not knowing if they'd welcome it. Until we're willing to be stretched, we'll never experience all God has for us. Growth requires stretching, just ask any pregnant woman. As we give birth to a new way of life, we'll experience lots of changes and challenges. I was just beginning my growing pains…

> WHAT GOD ASKS US TO DO, WE WILL BE ABLE, BUT WE MAY NOT BE COMFORTABLE.

Our YES leads to their YES

So there really is more. This encounter introduced me to a whole new way of living: listening and acting on the voice of the Holy Spirit. It has taken me on many crazy adventures with God, and I've grown to enjoy Him more and more through every situation.

As we listen and say YES to the promptings of God, we get to know Him better.

My sheep listen to my voice; I know them, And they follow me.
John 10:27 NIV

Listening is crucial to knowing. Learning to tune into the voice of the Spirit of God will lead you to know the Creator of the universe deeper. There is always deeper to go and more to know of God, He's an inexhaustible well. He'll whisper truth to you, guide you in decisions, and lead you to do some pretty crazy "out there" stuff which gives you a glimpse into His heart. When we say YES to God, it almost always involves someone else He cares about. Often, our YES is connected to another person's yes or breakthrough.

You know my friend I tried to avoid praying with? Well shortly after this, she voiced her desire to learn more about God and asked me about joining my small group. She quickly started attending and opened up about the health issues she'd been experiencing including headaches and neck problems. We covered her in prayer for healing and shared scriptures to give her hope and to declare over her situation. She began faithfully standing on the Word of God… then came the testimony.

A few weeks later, she could not contain herself, "Guys, you are never going to believe this! I've been praying and asking Jesus to heal me like He did with those in the Bible. I've been speaking the Word of God out. The doctor took an x-ray last week to see if there had been any improvement, and guess what?! My neck has been twisted miraculously back into place! God healed me! JESUS IS MY SAVIOR!" she declared. *Come on somebody?!* She experienced healing and her Savior! Isn't this the life we crave when we read the Bible stories of old? The disciples went around preaching the Good News and seeing the miraculous, why can't we?! This is the Kingdom.

Now, what if I had said NO when God asked me to pray for my friend instead of YES? What could have happened? I am a firm believer Christ can and will accomplish His plans with or without us, but He invites us to participate. If I had declined His request to pray for her, He could have asked another, and they would have seen the miracle of salvation and healing. But I would not have missed this for the world! Co-laboring with God to accomplish His work has got to be our driving force to say YES, even if it is hard. We *get* to do this.

This first YES showed me the outcome is worth the discomfort. I realized there's a chance agreeing to an opportunity with God may risk a relationship with another, but not with Him. It showed me my obedience might change someone's life forever, and I quickly learned I will probably be *able* but not always *comfortable*.

So if you decide to start saying YES, my first tip is: Be willing to be stretched. Am I saying you have to kiss your comfort zone goodbye forever? No, but will you be asked to leave it? Sometimes, yes. In those moments, it helps to consider who this yes will affect and how it will change their life, not only yours. People are waiting for us to say YES so they can experience God and so they too can say YES!

Just. Say. Yes.

STRETCHING YOUR YES

SCRIPTURE TO APPLY:
Here I am! I stand at the door and knock. If anyone hears my voice and opens the door, I will come in and eat with that person, and they with me. Revelation 3:20

SONG TO LISTEN:
"I Give You My Yes," John Michael Howell

QUESTIONS:
How do you know if it's the Holy Spirit speaking or if it is your own voice?

When the Lord asks, are you willing to step out of your comfort zone?

Share a time God asked you to do something uncomfortable for Him. Did you say yes or no? Explain.

CHALLENGE:
Make a pact with God to say YES when He comes knocking and be willing to open and walk through the door!

2

I'LL SAY YES
Even if...
I am scared

Well, this is going to be boring, I grimly said to myself after discovering our main pastor was not speaking at church that Sunday. (Tell me I'm not the only one who has entertained this fleshly thought!) While the disappointment set in, the speaker took the stage. I vividly remember expecting to be uninterested in the message when the Holy Spirit instantly interrupted my judgemental ways: *Don't discount him, I can speak through anyone I choose.* Talk about a spiritual gut punch. I think I needed it. This sentence has challenged me throughout the years to always have an open heart to whoever is sharing, whether they use eloquent and wise words or not, if they're famous or unknown. It makes me think of what God spoke to the prophet Samuel when he was sent to anoint the next King of Israel. At first, Samuel thought someone else would be a better leader than David, but the Spirit interrupted His judgemental thoughts, too.

But the LORD said to Samuel, "Don't judge by his appearance or height, for I have rejected him. The LORD doesn't see things the way you see them. People judge by outward appearance, but the LORD looks at the heart."
1 Samuel 16:7

I'LL SAY YES

After the needed correction of the Holy Spirit, I decided to listen with a teachable heart! And boy am I glad I did because this message has marked me forever. (Won't God do it?!) The pastor preached from 1 Corinthians 9 about running the race of faith as if to win the prize. During his timely message, I surmised, *At this rate, I ain't winning no prize!* Haha. True story. I started praying in the middle of service, *Lord, how can I run well for you? I am a stay-at-home mom, I can't go out to the highways and byways to preach the Good News! What can I do?!* He gave me two directives for that season.

One: Just write.
Two: Do what you can with what you have.

Okay, these instructions were something I could work with. Suddenly a picture flooded my mind, a memory of a balloon declaring "It's a Girl!" on a mailbox in my neighborhood, accompanied with an assignment—the next opportunity to say YES: "Bless this family with food like you do for your friends who have a baby."

Again, could I bring food to a new mama? Absolutely. This was completely within my ability! But the whole truth is I had no problem dropping off food to people I KNEW, not COMPLETE STRANGERS!!! *Come on, God.* While considering my YES, a light bulb switched on: *If I continue this pattern, I might never see my comfort zone again.* LOL.

After a little debating, I gave God my YES, with the condition I would be protected, and He would tell me exactly what to say. This world is full of interesting characters, so if God tells you to go to a stranger's house, you better know it was Him. By this time, I'd practiced hearing His voice and acting on it enough, experiencing confirmation after confirmation that I was confident of the command. I was steeped in His love and trusted His protection.

Our perspective and relationship with the Lord will determine what we do for Him. If I didn't trust Him completely, knowing He was good and was going to keep me safe, I would never have said YES to this assignment. I would have let fear stop me. I would have let culture tell me: You can't go to a stranger's house, they might hurt you. But I knew my God, and I knew His plans for me were for good and not harm (Jeremiah 29:11), I knew He was a loving Father and would protect me as His daughter. Which brings us back to an important truth from the parable of the talents. Our focus will be on the underlined portions.

> OUR PERSPECTIVE AND RELATIONSHIP WITH THE LORD WILL DETERMINE WHAT WE DO FOR HIM.

"After a long time the master of those servants came and settled accounts with them. The man who had received five talents approached, presented five more talents, and said, <u>'Master, you gave me five talents.</u> See, I've earned five more talents.'

"His master said to him, <u>'Well done, good and faithful servant!</u> You were faithful over a few things; I will put you in charge of many things. Share your master's joy.'

"The man with two talents also approached. He said, <u>'Master, you gave me two talents.</u> See, I've earned two more talents.'

"His master said to him, <u>'Well done, good and faithful servant!</u> You were

faithful over a few things; I will put you in charge of many things. Share your master's joy.'

'The man who had received one talent also approached and said, <u>'Master, I know you. You're a harsh man, reaping where you haven't sown and gathering where you haven't scattered seed. So I was afraid</u> and went off and hid your talent in the ground. See, you have what is yours.'

<u>"His master replied to him, 'You evil, lazy servant!"</u>

Notice the first two servants' responses to their master? They basically say, 'Master, you gave me this, so I did this...' their responses were identical (except for the amounts they had). But, look at what the third servant said. He added something to his response the other two did not: *I know you. You're a harsh man, reaping where you haven't sown and gathering where you haven't scattered seed. So I was afraid...* Hmmmmm. It seems this servant had a different perspective of the master than the first two, and because of this, he was "afraid." But, the funny thing is, this servant had the audacity to say, "I know you." This kind of makes me laugh because obviously he didn't (though he thought he did).

The parable highlights one result of our relationship with God, the master being the Father and the servants representing us. This little snippet gives us insight into how important our perspective and relationship with our Heavenly Father is. The third servant declares the master is harsh. The first two didn't say this, and perhaps this unveils the secret of why people are willing to say YES to God and why they are not... maybe those who refuse to seize the God-given opportunity don't really know Him that well. The servant who did nothing was scared and took the opportunity given him and buried it in the ground. How did the master react to being called harsh? He declares the servant is both wicked and lazy.

I think the first two servants knew the master in a different way, not because they said they knew Him, but because they showed they did—they took the opportunities He gave and ran with them. Perhaps they are the ones who truly knew the master and trusted Him. What was the result? The master praised them, *'Well done, good and faithful servant! You were faithful over a few things; I will put you in charge of many things. Share your master's joy.'*

I don't know about you, but I long for the day I hear the words, "Well done, good and faithful servant!" Although, I hope He replaces 'servant' with 'daughter!' I've even thought about what I want my gravestone to say. Is this too morbid? Maybe, but maybe not. If I could have a simple inscription describing my life I hope it can be said:

She said yes to God

Don't you want the halls of heaven to record your response to every opportunity God presented you with as "YES" every time? I think we will when we know our good, faithful, Father loves and adores us. He cares for us. He has a good plan for us, and we have got to trust Him fully to walk out our purpose.

Our YES, His Words

So, God does send people to the houses of absolute strangers. I can't leave you hanging, do you want to know what happened? I knew the Spirit was leading me to this family, and since I trusted God, I said YES and believed He would go with me.

I'LL SAY YES

And I went.

Strolling up to the front door, I clutched my bakery-bought, packaged loaf of bread (because who's going to be comfortable eating a homemade food item from a complete stranger, am I right?) and while inching closer, I prayed, *Okay, God, what do I even say to these people?* I had said YES, but I had not received further instructions on what to say when the door opened.

God replied calm and cool as ever, "I'll tell you when you get there." He gave me nothing—yet. I'm telling you Psalm 81:10, "Open wide your mouth and I will fill it," came more alive than ever, and I was standing on this promise!!

So, having no prepared speech, I reluctantly knocked on the front door. I had peace, but I wouldn't be telling the story accurately if I claimed to be fearless. I trusted God wouldn't send me to a crazy person's house, but I had to do it afraid. When the mom answered the door, I opened my mouth to speak, and the Holy Spirit met me there. "Hey, I know this may sound a little odd, but I just really felt like God was leading me to come and bring you this bread and meet you." And God did the rest. I gave Him my YES, and He filled my mouth with His words. As it turned out, they were Christians, and they had just launched a church, finances were tight, and as of that morning had just run out of bread. *Come on now!* I could not believe it. Her husband actually said: "This is our manna from Heaven!" I had heard of this happening on the mission field, but I had never been a part of the miraculous provision of God like this! I am still in awe that He used someone like me.

From then on, I began running the race of faith, in the way I could, with what I had. However, I would have never done this if I did not have a very close relationship with the Lord. This must be in place. Our perspective of God will determine what we do for Him—whether we are filled with love and trust, or doubt.

Remember how I mentioned our YES is connected to other yeses? Well, this couple was the first family who introduced us to "craft coffee." They opened up our coffee horizons which would come into play a little later in my journey, and you'll read about it in just a few chapters. Sometimes saying YES both blesses the other person and plays a part in your story in the long run. You never know what is on the other side of your YES to God. But He does.

Saying YES this time taught me that just because you agree to follow through doesn't mean the nerves automatically go away. Sometimes, we just have to "do it scared," but walking close with God—knowing His character and heart—gives us the confidence needed to do the hard things. Our relationship with the Lord determines what we're willing to do for Him.

If you've decided to say YES when God calls, here are a few tips I picked up from this experience. First and foremost: Get closer to Jesus. Spend time in His presence. Get to know His heart. Begin to identify His voice. Fall in love with Him. Learn how to trust Him. Knowing God well helps you both discern His voice and trust His character. We're willing to do just about anything for someone we know has our best interest at heart.

> KNOWING GOD WELL HELPS YOU BOTH DISCERN HIS VOICE AND TRUST HIS CHARACTER.

Second, just because fear is present, don't write off the opportunity. You can possess peace AND feel nervous at the same time. If you know the Holy Spirit is leading, do it anyway. Third, trust Him to give you the words when the time comes. Often, we want to have the exact words planned and rehearsed before we step out, but if you're going to be Spirit-led, He might send you somewhere with little to no notice, and in those scenarios, you will have to rely on what He gives you in the moment. Trusting He will show up and give us the right words at the right time will take us places and show us things we never thought possible.

Know God. Do it scared. Trust He'll give you the words.

STRETCHING YOUR YES

SCRIPTURE TO APPLY:
Don't worry how you'll respond, and don't worry what you should say. The Holy Spirit will give you the words to say at the moment when you need them. Luke 12:11b-12 VOICE

SONG TO LISTEN:
"No Fear," Kari Jobe

QUESTIONS:
How would you describe your relationship with God currently?

Do you ever let fear stop you from stepping out for Jesus?

What countermeasures can you put in place to overcome being afraid to say YES?

Share about a time when God showed up and spoke through you.

CHALLENGE:
Is there something you have been avoiding because of fear? Let the Devil know you aren't afraid anymore by asking God to fill you with His love and help you overcome this fear once and for all! If the Holy Spirit leads you to do something about it, step out and ask Him to fill you with the courage and the words to accomplish the task!

I'LL SAY YES
Even if...
I might get punched

You want me to do what? Standing in the jam-packed, sweaty New York City subway, hanging on to a pole for dear life—while simultaneously trying not to fall on anyone—God decides here of all places to ask me to do something uncomfortable.

"I said, tell her I love her." The response was crystal clear.

I knew this was God and not my idea because everyone knows there are certain unspoken rules of the NY subway:

1) Don't make eye contact with anyone
2) Mind your own business
3) Definitely don't speak to anyone
4) Keep your hands to yourself

Translation: I would not come up with this outrageous plan to break the subway rules and quite possibly get not only embarrassed but hurt. Here I was, already violating one and two, and now God was pushing me to go ahead and break rule number three. As I stood there trying my darndest to balance myself, a crowd of people had rushed in, and one young lady took a seat.

I noticed her right away, fiddling with her engagement ring and crying. I watched as tears streamed down her cheeks, but no one acknowledged her.

I don't know if it was the southern girl in me, the extreme extrovert, or my slightly rebellious nature, but I sensed I was about to disregard the 'subway rules.' I could feel the compassion of Jesus welling up inside me, and I didn't care what the "no-nos" of the subway were, I was about to cross the line. This is one of the reasons it is so important to spend time with the Lord and let Him fill your heart with His love. The more we're with Him, the more we become like Him. So, not only did I know He was telling me to give her a message of His love, I could actually feel His love for her. This is the difference between knowing and experiencing. *Knowing* about God in your mind is not the same as *experiencing* His power in your heart. Encountering the love of God literally transforms our hearts. I sensed this supernatural love was not originating from me because I didn't know this girl at all—but at that moment, it felt like I had known her all my life; You know why I felt this way about a stranger? While I had never met her, God had. He's known this girl her whole life, and as a vessel of His love, He was pouring His heart for her into mine. This is how we can minister to those we don't know; we don't rely on our experience with them, we rely on His.

> THE MORE WE'RE WITH HIM, THE MORE WE BECOME LIKE HIM.

To be truthful, I didn't say yes immediately. I saw this girl in her pain and wanted to act, but the flesh told me not to. Thoughts like: *What will others think? What is going to happen if I do? This girl might actually punch me—I mean this is New York City*, flooded my mind and chipped away at my confidence. But another phrase interrupted these thoughts:

"Tell her I love her." The directive of the Spirit and the feeling of His love would not go away.

The conductor announced the next stop was mine. *Stay safe or say yes?* The battle raged in my mind, but then, I wondered, *If I don't tell her that God loves her, what could happen?* And that was it. This was the question that broke the dam of fear holding me back from pouring out God's love. I had to take a risk because I couldn't waste this opportunity to be a voice of hope and truth, maybe the only one she'd hear.

As we approached the station, I mustered every ounce of courage I could, asked God to help me, and reached out and actually touched this complete stranger, *gasp*, well there went rule #4. She looked up at me through tear-stained eyes, and I said, "God told me to tell you that He loves you." And then I braced myself for the worst. To my relief, instead of a punch in the face, her tear-stained eyes were filled with gratitude, and she choked out the most earnest, "Thank you," I've ever heard in my life. I smiled, said, "You're welcome," and stepped off the train. I never saw her again.

Saying YES produces Joy

So joy is real. When my foot hit the station platform, my heart filled with inexplicable joy. Before I said YES and stepped out to encourage a complete stranger, I was hesitant and wrestled with God, but after I did what He asked, I was flooded with the joy of the Lord. This is what Jesus said would happen in John 15:10-11:

I'LL SAY YES

When you obey my commandments, you remain in my love, just as I obey my Father's commandments and remain in his love. I have told you these things so that you <u>will be filled with my joy</u>. Yes, your joy will overflow!

When we do as He asks, we are filled with joy. I used to read this verse like: if you don't obey every commandment of the Bible, you won't have joy. Which is literally impossible, and this interpretation left me feeling like I could never experience this kind of joy. But what if Jesus meant you'll have joy as you listen for the active voice of the Lord and follow as He commands? As I have listened and acted on the voice of the Holy Spirit, He has given me more and more to do, and each time, I experience overwhelming joy! It turns out saying YES to God does in fact lead to getting more Kingdom opportunities and produces more fruit of the Spirit in our lives. It's just one simple word: YES.

Remember how the master in the parable of the talents responded to the servants who made the most of every opportunity put in their path? Look what happened to those who said YES.

His master said to him, 'Well done, good and faithful servant! You were faithful over a few things; I will put you in charge of many things. <u>Share your master's joy.</u>'

There's joy again, it's real. When you say YES and do what God asks of you, you will experience your Master's joy—the joy of the Lord. The world tells us joy can be found in money, "likes," or even titles, but it's not found there. True, lasting joy comes from walking with God and partnering with Him and His agenda. If you're looking to possess a joy that never fades, it's found in listening and acting on the voice of the Holy Spirit. When you do what He says, His fruit manifests.

Saying YES on the subway taught me the world's unspoken rules mean nothing to God. Think of the stories of the good Samaritan, the woman at the well, and Zacheus. In each of those stories, the hero violated cultural norms by both engaging, accepting, and empowering a person with whom others weren't willing to associate. Jesus did not care about what others thought, He lived by what His Father thought and He's asking us to do the same. Could your YES risk your reputation? Good! It's probably God (if it's a positive, life-giving thing, obviously)! Jesus put His reputation on the line consistently to minister to sinners all the time and was even called a drunk Himself. He didn't care. He obeyed anyway. Jesus knew who He was and He knew His mission, His eyes were set like flint (Isaiah 50:7) on doing the will of the Father, and He is our leader.

> TRUE, LASTING JOY COMES FROM WALKING WITH GOD AND PARTNERING WITH HIM AND HIS AGENDA.

Ministering to a crying stranger in a questionable place unveiled another tip for saying YES: Forget what others think and embrace what God thinks of you AND the person He's calling you to bless. When we lift our eyes off ourselves and look to the needs of others, realizing their lives might hang in the balance, we gain a different perspective and motivation. Let our decisions alone be guided by doing the will of our Father.

Don't live by man's opinion, live by His.

STRETCHING YOUR YES

SCRIPTURE TO APPLY:
Am I now trying to win the approval of human beings, or of God? Or am I trying to please people? If I were still trying to please people, I would not be a servant of Christ. Galatians 1:10 NIV

SONG TO LISTEN:
"In Jesus Name," Katy Nichole

QUESTIONS:
Have you ever let cultural norms hinder you from being a witness? Share the circumstances.

If Jesus was willing to risk His life for you, would you be willing to take a risk for another? Explain your answer.

When the opinions of others threaten to stop you from saying YES, how can you overcome negative thoughts?

Share an experience where a stranger blessed you in your time of need.

CHALLENGE:
The next time you see someone in distress, stop and ask God, *Is there anything you want me to do or say to help?*

I'LL SAY YES

Even if...
I want to say no

Yeah, I don't really want to do that right now. I shot straight with God during the internal wrestling match taking place at a rest stop. I mean, can't I just go to the bathroom without having to say YES to a Kingdom opportunity?! Apparently not, and to my surprise, I ended up being glad this chance of partnering came at an inopportune time. This particular location had a concession stand of sorts, so naturally, my kids wanted some snacks and ice cream to make our road trip more bearable. As I was standing in line holding my sweet baby Jack, a young, ten-year-old boy came up to me and struck up a conversation.

He started with, "How old is your baby?" And he continued to drill me with questions until he blurted out, "I have a baby sister from my new mom. My real mom died last year." I detected sadness in his voice and could see it in his eyes. When this young boy went *there*, my ears were perked not only to what he was saying but to what the Spirit was doing. As our chat took a shortcut from shallow to the deep end, I knew the door had opened for ministry at a rest stop.

When discerning whether an opportunity is from God or not,

pay attention to the conversation. If you are shooting the breeze with a complete stranger and the interaction gets very deep very fast, it's a sure sign God is up to something. Does this happen often for you? I'm convinced that when someone spends a lot of time in the presence of God, His fragrance envelops us, and when we interact with others, we provide a supernatural safety net. People find a safe place in our presence to share their hurts, the same way we feel in the throne room of Heaven. This is why making time in the secret place must be a priority, not only for our own healing and regular restoration but so others can detect a safe Kingdom person. People often say to me, "I don't know why I am telling you this." But I know. It's not me who is making them feel at ease, it's God. They feel the refreshing wind of comfort; they smell the fragrance of Heaven.

When I recognized this young boy had revealed a wound in his life, I listened to him and Heaven—multitasking like a boss, I engaged and simultaneously asked the Lord if He wanted me to share anything with my new little friend.

"Tell him I love him and I see him," came the typical reply.

Hmmmmmm, well I don't really want to do that right now, I answered in a slightly snarky tone. Now, you may be wondering, why did I ask, if I didn't want to comply? I don't know. Maybe I was wishfully thinking God would have said, "Nothing, just listen." But it should not have surprised me when He replied with an uncomfortable instruction. So guess what I did guys? I said NO.

I chickened out, in front of a ten-year-old! True story. I felt pretty bad about it, too. As the proverbial rooster was crowing for the third time, I wondered if this is how Peter felt when he denied

Jesus in front of a young girl on the night of His betrayal. I quickly escaped the situation and hid in the bathroom. Then, the guilt really hit. *What if this little boy needed to hear about God's love today? What if it changes his life? What if it comforted him to know that even though his earthly mother was gone, His Heavenly Father was here for him?*

Then and there, I renewed my vow to the Lord. *Okay, I know I agreed to always say YES, but I messed up there. I am sorry I chickened out. If you have me run into that little boy again, I will tell him, I promise.* Part of me hoped I would never have to make good on that promise, but if by some miracle he was put right in front of me, I would KNOW God wanted me to tell this young man how much He loved him.

Ever heard the phrase: "Slow obedience is no obedience"? Well, Biblically, this isn't necessarily true. Now, I do believe there are appointed windows of time and we could miss out on blessings if we don't instantly follow… but, if we are asked by God to do something and we say no at first, or push it off for a time, this doesn't mean we're out of fellowship with Him or that He won't give us another chance. Look at Peter, after publicly denying Jesus, he was restored and got to preach the first message of the Church, and 3,000 people got saved! God can still use us, even if we feel we've let Him down. I want to set someone free from the guilt of delaying to obey. God is ready to restore. He is willing to give you a second and third chance. Don't believe me? Check out these words from the mouth of Jesus in Matthew 21:28-31, emphasis added:

"But what do you think about this? A man with two sons told the older boy, 'Son, go out and work in the vineyard today.'

I'll SAY YES

The son answered, 'No, I won't go,' but later he changed his mind and went anyway.

Then the father told the other son, 'You go,' and he said, 'Yes, sir, I will.' But he didn't go.

"Which of the two obeyed his father?"

They replied, "The first."

Then Jesus explained his meaning: "I tell you the truth, corrupt tax collectors and prostitutes will get into the Kingdom of God before you do."

Well if this doesn't mess with the "only immediate obedience is acceptable" mentality! Jesus was not mincing words. This story encouraged me so much since I'm not always the "fastest at the draw" when it comes to obeying. If at first, we resist what has been asked of us, as long as we eventually say YES, we're still doing what our Father wants, even if it was delayed. We serve a God who offers a second chance! We don't want to be looped in with the second son, declaring we will say YES and obey perfectly, but when it comes down to it, don't follow through. We want to emulate the first, who after weighing the obstacles, possible outcomes, and our own feelings, may wrestle with obedience at first, eventually, we change our mind and say YES! Let us be the ones who follow through!

Even though I didn't say YES instantly at that rest stop, I was determined to say YES if given another chance. Exiting the restroom, I spotted Andrew and the kids enjoying ice cream on a nearby bench. This was a rare occurrence, as we NEVER "hang out" at rest stops—we are in and out, and even try to do it in record time. The fact that my husband was like, "Let's just sit here and not rush," was a miracle in and of itself. I just wanted to jump in the car, ensuring there would be no way I would have to speak to the little boy, but surely they had left by now anyway. I relaxed, took a seat… and guess who walked by? My young friend and his entire family. I was frozen. *I'm not going to do it now, not in front of his family. Forget that.*

I did not get up. I could not get up. This was more than I bargained for. I said I would tell HIM, not his whole crew, now adults and siblings were involved. You know what happened next? This family had the audacity to get in their car and not leave. If you could have heard my thoughts at this moment it sounded a little like: *Are you kidding me? Just pull away, people!! I am trying to avoid obeying God!* I'm so godly, as you can see. This family did not respond to my internal commands. It was almost as if God was having them wait until I obeyed. Won't He do it?!

While I believe delaying my YES wasn't considered flat-out disobedience, it did have a consequence. Before I only had to share His message with one; because I waited, now more onlookers were involved. Perhaps saying YES the first time we're asked will make the assignment easier than if we wait! God uses it all for our good and His glory, but there are definite benefits of obeying quickly!

> PERHAPS SAYING YES THE FIRST TIME WE'RE ASKED WILL MAKE THE ASSIGNMENT EASIER THAN IF WE WAIT!

The Lord kept tugging, so VERY reluctantly I got up from the bench and headed toward the car. Boy, did it feel incredibly awkward, and boy, did I wish I had listened to God earlier when it was just the one young man, instead of an audience—including parents who might not receive my God or my message. I didn't know what this family was going to think, but because I cared what God thought more than anything, I went.

Though I was sweating bullets, I marched up to the van, knocked on the window, and a woman slowly rolled it down. I took a deep breath and delivered the message, "Hello! I was just chatting with your son back there at the snack bar. Hey buddy! And as we were talking, I felt the need to tell him that God loves him and He sees him." And I awaited their response.

"Wow! Thank you so much for coming up and telling us!"

Then, I followed with, "As a matter of fact He loves all of you! He wanted you to know that today." They all smiled and thanked me and I blessed them on their journey. I was so glad I listened and acted. I didn't really want to at first, but I saw how much God loved that boy and his family and I got to tell them.

Say YES and see His heart

So God is really after people. My rest stop encounter showed me He cares for everyone, no matter how old or young. He values those we may sometimes overlook, and this reminds me of one final thing I want to point out from the parable we've been unpacking.

For it is just like a man about to go on a journey. <u>*He called his own servants and entrusted his possessions to them.*</u> *To one he gave five talents, to another two talents, and to another one talent, depending on each one's ability. Then he went on a journey.* When God asks us to say YES to Him, it always has to do with His possessions, and what are His most valuable possessions? People. His heart is for people. He loves people. Every time I say YES to God, people are involved.

God is looking for those He can entrust to care for people. And, as you can see in my rest stop mission, the object of His love was not someone I would typically walk up to and share Good News. The people who are close to His heart may not look like we expect, and ministering may very well shift our plans, but we have to be open to this. This is exactly the attitude Jesus modeled.

> GOD IS LOOKING FOR THOSE HE CAN ENTRUST TO CARE FOR PEOPLE.

Jesus was the most important person to ever walk the planet, and just about every time He was doing anything, someone showed up on the scene to disrupt Him. Jesus, though the greatest of all, was never rushed, out of sorts, or frustrated to have His journey delayed to minister to the hurting. Why? Because He knew the heart of the Father was for people, and His mission was all about the saving of souls.

How Jesus treated people has marked me. If the One whom the world was made through, by, and for—the actual King of the earth, the most significant human to ever live—always made Himself available to the Father and frequently allowed His plans to seemingly be delayed, then who am I to do any less? I'm certainly not more important than Jesus and neither are "my plans." God's plan is what matters, and the more I realize He might (and often does) have a different agenda for my day, when I make myself available to the leading of the Holy Spirit, I'm not as frustrated when my schedule goes awry.

I think one of the reasons Jesus was willing to minister to whoever was in His path was because His heart was full of love for humanity, and God wants to fill our hearts with His *agape* love for people, too. The agape love of God must first be experienced in order for us to pour it out. We cannot give what we don't have. We won't be able to share what we've never experienced. I talk a lot about this in my first book, *The Awesome One*, because to give love, we must possess love. If you have a hard time really loving and ministering to people, I want you to know I used to be this way.

I used to be very judgemental, and I wasn't full of compassion at all. God gently told me so, one day. But, all it took for my heart to change, was a simple prayer, *God can you teach me how to really love people?* That was it. He said YES to my heartfelt request and started to fill me with His love and compassion. So if you want to love people more and you're not sure how, just ask God to help you in this area. If you want to be more available to God's plans, ask the Father to give you a willing heart to submit to His agenda daily. When the compassion of God and submission to His will takes root in our hearts, we can't help but say YES, ministering and blessing those to whom the Spirit leads us.

Maybe like my first reaction to God's directive at the rest stop, you sometimes hesitate to say YES. Want to know what helps? Prioritizing the possible outcome. Elevating the needs of the other person ahead of ours can change our motivation and perspective. When we consider the consequences of *not* saying YES, they often far outweigh the potentially awkward twenty seconds for us. I mean, we can do just about anything for this amount of time; twenty seconds isn't long at all.

- What if those seconds could change someone's story?
- What if it could prevent them from making a permanent solution to a temporary problem?
- What if it breathes purpose into their life?
- What if it introduces them to their Savior?

Pondering these questions builds our courage to risk our comfort and potentially impact their life forever.

God is trying to get His Kingdom reigning in every part of our hearts, bodies, and minds. When we look like Heaven, smell like Heaven, have the heart of Heaven, and react in a Heavenly way, we represent Heaven accurately to those around us. This requires us to listen as the Holy Spirit leads, do what He says, and allow Him to transform our hearts and renew our minds. Letting all of Him fill all of us.

The rest stop adventure showed me when we say YES, we encounter more of God and more of His heart for people. As we partner with God in His mission, we're also showing Him we can be entrusted with His possessions. This YES began showing me who He valued, and I was a little surprised. The world teaches us to value the rich, the famous, and the important, while Jesus said, "Let the children come to me, and do not hinder them, for the Kingdom of Heaven belongs to such as these," in Matthew 19:14 NIV. It also displayed the grace and mercy of my God. He wasn't removing His favor from me or breaking

> WHEN WE LOOK LIKE HEAVEN, SMELL LIKE HEAVEN, HAVE THE HEART OF HEAVEN, AND REACT IN A HEAVENLY WAY, WE REPRESENT HEAVEN ACCURATELY TO THOSE AROUND US.

our relationship because I didn't obey right away, He's a God of second chances. *And all God's people said, "AMEN!"* We're not out of the game if we said no or delayed obeying. There is forgiveness, restoration, and another opportunity, we need only ask for another chance!

Here are a few tips I picked up in my rest area ministry. First, pay attention to the conversation, and if it takes an unusually deep turn, intentionally ask God if He is doing something. Second, if you bail out, you can ask God for another chance. But the best tip I have for delaying a YES is don't do it! While God opened the door a second time, I also learned a valuable lesson: it is way easier if we say YES the first time. Lastly, ask the Spirit to refresh you with the fragrance of Heaven. As a person sent from God to change and impact culture, accurately represent His Kingdom. God is well able to breathe on you in a fresh way so as you minister people can feel the Heaven in you.

Evaluate conversations and God's plan. Say YES the first time. Ask for another chance. Pray for a fresh wind.

STRETCHING YOUR YES

SCRIPTURE TO APPLY:
But thanks be to God, who always leads us in triumph in Christ, and through us reveals the fragrance of the knowledge of Him in every place.
2 Corinthians 2:14 NASB

SONG TO LISTEN:
"Fresh Wind/What A Beautiful Name," Hillsong Worship

QUESTIONS:
Would you walk up to a stranger and tell them God loves them? Why or why not?

Do you value all people as much as God does? Or just some people?

What is one practical way you can continually pursue transforming your heart into the heart of our Heavenly Father?

Share about a time God gave you a second chance.

CHALLENGE:
Ask the Holy Spirit to fill your heart with God's love… and the next time you can feel God's love for another person, tell them!

LIVING INTERRUPTED

Making myself available to God was the first leg of my journey. Each YES brought more fire. Every time I acted on the leading of the Holy Spirit, He poured out a little more oil, a little more fuel, and before I knew it, my heart went from barely glowing embers to a blazing bonfire. If you want to be "more on fire for God," saying YES when He leads is the path to ignite your flame. Perhaps *this* is how we take up our cross and follow Jesus: We die to our plans and go where He leads. It doesn't seem like dying to our agenda would be abundant living, but blessings from the Lord often come in unexpected packaging. I used to despise having my plans altered unexpectedly—but this changed when I found a treasure hidden within a familiar Bible story. Let's read it now.

Then an expert in the law stood up to test him, saying, "Teacher, what must I do to inherit eternal life?"

"What is written in the law?" he asked him. "How do you read it?"

He answered, "Love the Lord your God with all your heart, with all your soul, with all your strength, and with all your mind;" and "your neighbor as yourself."

"You've answered correctly," he told him. "Do this and you will live."

But wanting to justify himself, he asked Jesus, "And who is my neighbor?"

Jesus took up the question and said: "A man was going down from Jerusalem to Jericho and fell into the hands of robbers. They stripped him, beat him up, and fled, leaving him half dead. A priest happened to be going down that road. When he saw him, he passed by on the other side. In the same way, a Levite, when he arrived at the place and saw him, passed by on the other side.

But a Samaritan on his journey came up to him, and when he saw the man, he had compassion. He went over to him and bandaged his wounds, pouring on olive oil and wine. Then he put him on his own animal, brought him to an inn, and took care of him. The next day he took out two denarii, gave them to the innkeeper, and said, 'Take care of him. When I come back I'll reimburse you for whatever extra you spend.'

"Which of these three do you think proved to be a neighbor to the man who fell into the hands of the robbers?"

"The one who showed mercy to him," he said.

Then Jesus told him, "Go and do the same."
Luke 10:25-37 CSB

Well, God did it again. As I read through the very familiar story of The Good Samaritan, it prompted me to ask the question: Am I willing to live interrupted? Notice how the story mentions, *But a Samaritan on his journey came up to him…*? Let's put ourselves in the story. Imagine we're on a road trip with our family, we have a set timeline, a non-refundable hotel room booked, and pre-paid tickets reserved at an attraction… and suddenly, a stranger needs our help. Are we willing to delay our plans in order to bless another? What if it changes our whole vacation? What if it costs us money? But… What if it alters the course of someone's life?

While preparing to write this section of the book, I knew part of my YES journey involved a willingness to be interrupted, so I began typing these very words to encourage you… and on that very day, God prompted a woman all the way across the world to confirm this is God's way. Check out what author and speaker Lana Vawser said:

"We must be happily interruptible. Let us live lives so surrendered, yielded and sensitive to His leading, burning with first love fire, that we are ones who embrace the divine interruptions of God. Let us not hold tightly to "our way" but surrender it daily and live lives committed to His way, His plan, His timing and His agenda."[1]

Well if that wasn't timely. I'll be honest, historically, I haven't always been the first to be 'happily interruptible,' but after I saw the famous parable with a new perspective, God challenged me to be more willing to exchange my plans for His, as anyone who commits to saying YES must. May we start to see an interruption in a new light, as surprise Kingdom assignments. So I ask: Are you willing to live interrupted?

5

I'll Say Yes
Even if...
I don't want to

Did you give this message to the wrong person? I objected when God asked me to bless someone who had deeply wounded me. Oh, I argued on this one. Come on, don't tell me I'm the only one who occasionally pushes back when God gives a command I don't want to comply with?! I'm honest enough to admit I don't always gladly say YES as soon as He asks. I definitely did not give my YES as quickly the time He asked me to both forgive and send a blessing to someone who had ripped my heart out.

The directive dropped in my spirit during my quiet time. The floor was soaked with my tears, as I lay face down on the floor while singing, "I Surrender." I meant what I was singing. *Lord, I surrender, to your will, to your way, to your plan.* I meant it until His plan veered from mine.

His voice was clear as crystal: "Go get a card, and write a note, blessing the one who hurt you."

My response? You saw it above. *I mean seriously, did this message get mixed up in the heavenlies and mistakenly get delivered to the wrong person? No, like no. Not happening.*

I kept going... *Lord, did you mean to give this instruction to her? Just to remind you: She. Hurt. Me. So maybe she needs to be sending me the blessing, and an apology while she's at it. And by the way, I've already forgiven her, so why the blessing? Why can't I just forgive from a distance with no further contact?* Oh, I was arguing my case, y'all, and saying anything I could to deter Him from the directive He'd given me. This was most definitely an unwelcome interruption to my time in the secret place.

But He would not relent, "I said get out a card, write her a note, and bless her."

Ughhhhhh. I don't want to.

"But didn't you just say 'I Surrender?' Did you mean it or not? Are you going to surrender to my will or not?"

> SOMETIMES SAYING YES INVOLVES SURRENDERING TO HIS WILL ABOVE OUR OWN AND BLESSING THOSE WHO'VE HURT US.

What could I say? Did I just lie to the God of the universe, claiming with one breath I surrender to His will, but in another, declare no I am not going to do what He asks?! How could I not say YES, even if I did not want to? While sometimes saying YES involves telling people about Jesus, blessing strangers, spreading the love of God, and healing the hurting through a heartfelt word, sometimes saying YES involves surrendering to His will above our own and blessing those who've hurt us.

Something about our commitment to following the Lord

involves *forgiving* and sometimes also *blessing* those who've hurt us. If we want the Spirit of God to have full reign in our lives, if He prompts us to bless those who've hurt us, we can't neglect this YES. Why? Because God is after our wholeness and He knows what it will take to put us back together.

So, what did I do? Reluctantly, I said YES. I tracked down a blank notecard, fumbled through the catch-all drawer for a pen, and I sat down to write… but what to say? *Lord, I have no blessing for her, I've got some other things I could say though* (my comment laced with bitterness was a sure sign I'd not fully forgiven her). Then, a Bible verse flashed in my mind. I quickly penned the words, followed with well wishes and a prayer of blessing for her family. The truth is even though she had hurt me, I really did hope she was doing well. I never wish evil on others, no matter how they have treated me. I always want to let people know when they are on the heart of God and to encounter His love. It's been my experience that those who treat others poorly don't know how much God loves them—otherwise, they wouldn't act terribly.

Sometimes we wonder, "Would the Lord really ask me to show kindness to someone who'd hurt me so deeply?" Well, let's look at what Jesus says about this.

But I say unto you, <u>Love your enemies, bless them</u> that curse you, <u>do good to them</u> that hate you, and <u>pray for them</u> which despitefully use you, and persecute you… Matthew 5:44 KJV, emphasis added.

Love? Bless? Do good? Pray for them? At first glance, this seems like cruel and unusual punishment. It also feels like an impossible task, and it is, without the strength of our Savior. This is where God gets to shine. Anytime He asks us to do something impossible, we must remember it is not without His help. He wants to display His strength through our inability, His power through earthen vessels. This is the glory of God. His power manifested through us. Learning how to forgive and be a blessing to those who have treated us wrong is a lesson we can learn from the parable of the Good Samaritan.

<u>A man was going down from Jerusalem to Jericho</u> and fell into the hands of robbers. They stripped him, beat him up, and fled, leaving him half dead. A priest happened to be going down that road. When he saw him, he passed by on the other side. In the same way, a Levite, when he arrived at the place and saw him, passed by on the other side. <u>But a Samaritan on his journey came up to him, and when he saw the man, he had compassion. He went over to him and bandaged his wounds, pouring on olive oil and wine.</u>

It can be assumed the man going on his journey was a Jew, as Jesus was speaking to a Jewish crowd, and the man in the story was traveling from Jerusalem. You would think a Jewish Priest or Levite, who both served God in the temple would stop to help the hurting… but, oh no… they aren't the ones who offered a hand. It was a Samaritan. This would have been significant to a Jewish audience as they despised Samaritans, and it is important to the story because the Samaritan would have known this Jewish man probably didn't like him at all. Maybe the victim had once insulted the Samaritan, but it looks like the Samaritan knew about forgiveness and practiced it. He did not let a culture that consistently snubbed his people keep him from being a blessing. The Samaritan did not let the actions of others determine his behavior. This unlikely hero still blessed a person who potentially hated him. This is miraculous forgiveness and compassion, and it takes help from Heaven to accomplish.

Forgiving those who've hurt us is often insurmountable without divine intervention. But if Jesus could say, "Father, forgive them, for they don't know what they are doing" (Luke 23:24) while He was being murdered, and if He is in us, we can forgive those who've wronged us through His strength. We can and will forgive our persecutors—because we can do all things through CHRIST who strengthens us (Philippians 4:13). It is His power flowing through us!!

Now, I must point out that giving forgiveness, blessing, and kindness to those who have hurt us does not mean we always welcome everyone back into our life. We can forgive, love, and bless from a distance, while still having healthy boundaries. Forgiveness does not always equal restoration of relationship, although it can. This is something to bring before the Lord, trusted loved ones, and wise counsel. Always seek wisdom when walking through forgiveness and restoration.

YES ushers in Compassion

So you can overflow with compassion. I'm going to come clean: Before I blessed my old friend, I had no compassion for her. None. Nada. Out of obedience alone, I wrote the card, found her address, and stomped down the driveway, slightly against my will, to place the letter in the mail. Just as I went to put it in the mailbox, I kid you not, a huge gust of wind came and blew it out of my hand. (Ask me how many times that's ever happened, before or since! Zero.) To which I exclaimed, "Not today, Satan!" I *was* going to follow through with what God told me to do, and I *was not* going to let anything prevent me from completing this task. Not my reluctance and not the Devil. I fetched the letter, slammed the door shut, and raised the mailbox flag—signaling my surrender.

I'LL SAY YES

Okay, Lord, I did it. Not sure why, but I obeyed. I knew this was of God, because my offended flesh did not want to, and the truth is, in that moment I didn't feel anything, other than the satisfaction of knowing I had listened.

A few days later, something happened that I did not expect. I got a message from the girl I reluctantly blessed. She thanked me and told me how much my words had ministered to her, and then asked me if I had known about the cancer. *Cancer? What?* I had not known. She went on to tell me that she received the note on the very day she was having surgery to remove her cancer and how God displayed His love through my words.

Only God knew the whole story, only God could have known the exact day I needed to write and send the note. He knew, and He pushed my stubborn self to do what I didn't want to do because He knew the ministry which was about to take place. I burst into tears. The timing and the plans of the Lord are perfect.

Don't tell me "God doesn't still talk to people." I say *bull* to that. I have seen too much to believe this lie now. I have seen Him move in the lives of others, and I've seen Him move in mine, changing me through circumstances I would never and could never have orchestrated for myself.

Two things happened in me when I got the message from the estranged friend:

1) My confidence in my ability to hear from God was restored
2) My heart was filled with compassion and forgiveness for this woman

What I have not mentioned up to this point is: When this story took place, I was in a pit of deep spiritual depression. This lady I was prompted to bless previously told me *God was opposing me*, which made me question if I could hear His voice and if I was walking with Him. For a long time after that conversation, I wrestled with confidence in my faith. When someone says, "The Lord told me to tell you…" it puts a lot of weight into the next words out of their mouth. This is why I recommend using those words very cautiously.

When I wrote the letter, I wasn't trying to prove anything. I didn't even want to do it, for goodness sake! But God knew what I needed better than I did. First, not only did He all but make me bless this woman, but in doing so, the Lord showed both of us He *was* with me, and I *could* still hear from Him. I wasn't expecting this. I wasn't looking for this. I was simply saying YES. While the blessing was for her, it was also a confirmation to me. God Himself vindicated me like only He can.

Second, my heart was completely changed toward this lady after this interaction. My heart was flooded with the compassion of the Lord when I heard of her condition. I would never wish sickness or hurt on another, and when I learned of her suffering, I was filled with love, and once the love came in and melted my hard heart, I could finally forgive. The blessing was the final piece needed to solve my unforgiveness problem. I completely let it all go and fully forgave.

I believe sometimes we can forgive and never have to do anything else, but other times, we may need to bless someone in order to have full forgiveness envelop our hearts. Notice from my story, my old friend did not apologize or ask for forgiveness. She never has. But I still genuinely forgave her. If we are waiting for an apology to release hurt, that may never happen and we may never let it go. We must learn to forgive without an apology… if we can do that, there is no wound that can keep us chained down.

Believe it or not, something like this happened to Job in the Bible. Many of us are familiar with the pain and loss of Job, but how familiar are we with the restoration, and what led to it? Let's get a refresher. Job suffered terrible tragedies, and shortly after he had some "friends" arrive on the scene who, with their inaccurate words, added insult to injury. They did not bring encouragement but instead pulled Job further down. God didn't like it. But look what He asks Job to do for his "friends."

After the LORD had finished speaking to Job, he said to Eliphaz the Temanite: "I am angry with you and your two friends, for you have not spoken accurately about me, as my servant Job has. So now take seven bulls and seven rams and <u>go to my servant Job and sacrifice a burnt offering for yourselves. My servant Job will pray for you,</u> and I will accept his prayer and not deal with you according to your folly. You have not spoken the truth about me, as my servant Job has."

<u>*When Job prayed for his friends, the LORD restored his fortunes.*</u> *In fact, the LORD gave him twice as much as before!* Job 42:7-8, 10, emphasis added

Now, we don't have a record of Job's thoughts at this moment, but if you'll allow me some creative liberty, I have a guess. I mean if I was Job, I would have thought:

Do what?! I gotta pray for them? Lord! They. Discouraged. Me. Shouldn't they pray for me, shouldn't they bless me?

Maybe Job was more godly than I; let's be real, he probably was. We don't know what Job thought, but we do know what he did. Because God said it, He did it. Job prayed for his friends (who didn't deserve it) and then restoration came! Perhaps it is the same for us? Maybe God is calling us to pray for and bless the very ones who discouraged and hurt us so we can live fully restored, fully free.

Saying YES this time taught me when we've been hurt, it's important to ask God the strategy to walk out our full forgiveness. Forgiving looks different for everyone. For some, it will be a one-time: *I forgive them,* and it is released. For others, it may be a daily declaration of forgiveness until we actually feel it. Sometimes, there will be an action step. This could be sending them a message or it could mean going to a counselor or therapist. We might need to bless those who've offended us out loud every time we think of them, or we may start praying for them by name… each wound is unique, so we're going to need a tailor-made strategy from our loving Savior to experience complete healing from the hurt.

This lesson in forgiveness and blessing gave me a few tips to pass on. If you've committed to living interrupted, then you better be all-in. God is after complete wholeness, and often, He asks us to do the hardest things, with His assistance. First, seek and accept His help when the directive is beyond your capacity. Second, trust the timing of the Lord. I'm glad I didn't delay this YES because I would have missed the window. Could God have restored and filled me with compassion at a later time? Sure. But why wait?! Commit to getting your heart whole and your hurts mended so you can get on with your Kingdom work! Third, forgive and bless, show mercy and grace as much as you can. This guards your heart against bitterness and hate.

Rely on His strength. Have faith in His timing. Forgive and bless.

STRETCHING YOUR YES

SCRIPTURE TO APPLY:
Be kind and compassionate to one another, forgiving each other, just as in Christ God forgave you.
Ephesians 4:32 NIV

SONG TO LISTEN:
"I Surrender," Hillsong Worship & TAYA

QUESTIONS:
Is there any part of your life you need to surrender to God? Share what and why.

Has anyone hurt you that you still need to forgive? What is holding you back?

Healthy boundaries are necessary. Name some practical ways you can bless a person without giving them full access to your life.

Tell about a time when you blessed someone who had treated you poorly.

CHALLENGE:
It's time for heart work. Saying YES when it involves helping others can be so fulfilling, but we can't neglect our own hearts. This week, get alone with the Father and ask Him to reveal anyone in your life you need to forgive and/or bless.

6

I'll Say Yes

Even if...
I am unqualified

They want us to do what? I was in shock when the pastors of our church approached and asked us to lead the Small Group ministry years ago. I could think of every reason in the book why my husband and I weren't qualified for this position. We had no pastoral degree, were not accredited by any denomination, and I was a stay-at-home mom, while Andrew worked full time in construction—what did we know about leading a ministry? I was just happy to be attending a life-giving church and had not expected this interruption to my normal church-going plans. I was honored to even be considered, but also doubted I had what it took to lead well.

Our pastoral leadership was so healthy, empowering, and open-handed. They loved well and led well. They modeled servant leadership and called out potential in us before we saw it in ourselves. I learned so much from them during this season, and lessons they taught me have impacted everything I have done since. After much prayer and a little reluctance, we agreed to give it a try. Andrew and I said YES to spearheading a ministry we had never (on paper) been trained to lead. We threw ourselves into growing the "City Groups," as they were called at our church, and in spite of our un-qualifications, we started to see God's grace was sufficient in our weakness.

I prayed A LOT, started devouring books on how to have an effective Bible study community, we toured thriving churches across the country and met with their Small Group pastors—gleaning ALL the wisdom we could—and we developed our own program of training, equipping, and launching healthy small groups. I quickly found out I loved ministry.

Suddenly, I found myself in unknown territory. I was entrusted to make the final call on the material group leaders chose and had to have tough conversations when things didn't line up Biblically. As a person who used to avoid confrontation at all costs, I was forced to overcome this fear and discovered that when you invite God into difficult discussions, He shows up and provides the words. Older men and women were coming to us with questions and for training, looking to us to lead, all the while our eyes were fixed on Jesus, our Good Shepherd to guide us, so we could! I was completely humbled and a bit surprised to be respected for my position. Even though some knew we weren't the most qualified, they still honored us. It blessed me and taught me the beautiful lesson of always honoring authority, even if I thought someone else would be a better fit to lead.

My confidence as a leader grew in that season. We were taught how to lead by serving, not demanding everyone to serve our vision alone, but we empowered theirs. We cultivated a teachable environment, where it was safe to give and receive corrections. I learned how to have healthy confrontation, which is something I used to shy away from. My appreciation and need for the Holy Spirit grew as well. Occasionally, I wouldn't know the best course of action, and then a solution would pop in my head, and as I began to advise, He just spoke right through me. My mouth was moving but the words and knowledge were coming from somewhere else. I would get done and think: *WOW! God, thank you for showing up and dropping your wisdom, you are so cool!*

What I quickly learned from saying YES to leading a ministry I had no training for is you don't have to have all the qualifications or answers to walk out your calling; you just need the One who does. It is true He doesn't call the qualified, He qualifies those He calls. And I am living proof.

> OUR JOB IS TO SAY YES, AND GOD BRINGS US WHAT WE NEED WHEN WE NEED IT.

Our job is to say YES, and God brings us what we need when we need it. When our availability meets His ability, it's a life-changing experience.

Our YES, His Strength

So Christ can help us do all things. After a few months of leading small groups, our pastor started asking Andrew and me to occasionally lead the "team time" devotional. We only had one service at the time, so those volunteering would not get to attend the worship experience. Team time was the only church message they'd get for the day, no pressure or anything. *Yeah right!* I felt pressure. If you could have been a fly on the wall of my mind the first day I spoke, the struggle was REAL and so were the nerves! But, in spite of the butterflies in my stomach, I remembered an arrangement I had with Jesus (yes, we have another one, a few actually): *I am willing to get up and speak as long as you come with me and help me!* He always holds up His end of the bargain.

I'LL SAY YES

So I got up to share, again and again, and so did God. He always gave me the message, the words, and the courage. Then came something I NEVER expected. Our pastors were going to be gone one weekend during our "At The Movies" series… and the lead pastor asked me to host the ENTIRE SERVICE. This included everything but the message y'all. The opening prayer, the announcements, the offering, the close.

"Ummmmmmmmmmmm do what now?!" I absolutely questioned Pastor Jason, and said, "Well, let me pray about it."

He didn't blink an eye and replied, "Amber, you don't need to pray about it, you can do this."

I could not believe I was being asked to lead the service in place of the pastor or another staff member. I did not feel qualified and I did not feel worthy. I had attended churches where women didn't really say anything on the stage, and I had even been the object of gossip by pastoral leadership in the past. I didn't know what to do with pastors who believed I could lead in their stead. The acceptance and empowerment by Pastors Jason and Nicole were what my wounded heart needed. Remember in the parable of the Good Samaritan, the traveler had been beaten up by bandits and thieves? Life will do that. Even church folk, friends, and family can wound us. How did the Good Samaritan react to the person who was hurt?

A man was going down from Jerusalem to Jericho and fell into the hands of robbers. They stripped him, beat him up, and fled, leaving him half dead… But a Samaritan, as he traveled, came where the man was; and <u>when he saw him, he took pity on him. He went over to him and bandaged his wounds, pouring on olive oil and wine.</u> Then he put him on his own animal, brought *him to an inn, and took care of him.*

The Samaritan was filled with compassion and took from his own resources to clean and start the healing process of the wounds. Wow. This is what healthy leadership does. They aren't looking for people to serve them, they serve those they lead. They know when their people get stronger, the organization gets healthier. They get the magnificent privilege of helping the broken find healing. This is what my leaders did for me in this season. They loved, encouraged, and empowered me to heal.

Back to the difficult decision of whether I'd lead the service or not: I wanted to say NO, but y'all know God pressed me to accept this opportunity. So I said YES on the spot and was nervous for the whole week prior. Truly. I rehearsed my lines each day leading up to the service. Every time I pictured myself walking on stage, mic in hand, and all eyes on me, I was a WRECK. I was determined to not let angst win the battle of my nerves, God was with me after all, and His grace was enough! I also knew the power of speaking out the Word as a weapon to fight off jitters. Each time I imagined leading the service and the nerves began waging war on my body I combatted it with scripture:

"I can do ALL things through Christ who gives me strength. And ALL things include leading a service!" I repeated Philippians 4:13 like a broken record until Sunday arrived. I declared it up until the moment I took the stage, and when I started to speak, guess what happened? I crashed and burned. Just kidding, that would have been really bad. What really went down was I opened my mouth wide and HE filled it with good things like He promised He always would. I was shocked when people came up to me afterward exclaiming "how comfortable I seemed!" I was VERY uncomfortable before I took the stage, but once the Spirit started doing His thing through me, I was filled with comfort by the Comforter. Truly Jesus had given me His strength, His very Spirit.

I was so grateful for the opportunity, but more importantly, I was grateful for the leaders who called out potential in me when I didn't see it in myself. This is the type of leader I want to be—which is why some of my closest friends make jokes about how being my friend means you will be doing stuff you don't want to do—because I know what happens to people on the other side of their circle of comfort: breakthrough, healing, and purpose.

Sometimes, the YES the Lord requires of us will cause an element of discomfort. I think we've established God-opportunities almost always do, but we have to remember just because we feel unqualified, untrained, or not worthy—it doesn't mean we're not "the one" for the job.

Often, we look at our ability or inability when determining whether we'll do something for God. But I don't think He is looking at the same things we are. Remember, He doesn't think like we do, and His paths to restoration look much different than how we imagine they should go.

"For my thoughts are not your thoughts, neither are your ways my ways," declares the LORD. Isaiah 55:8 NIV

It's not our ability God needs; it is our availability. He's looking for those who aren't focused on qualifications but trust in His ability to qualify and strengthen the willing.

This YES taught me to trust the Holy Spirit to empower me for ministry. I learned when things are over my head to ask: Am I in Christ and is Christ in me? *Yes.* Well, then do I believe I can do ALL things through Jesus who is my strength? *Yep.* So, do I have faith that God can do it through me? *Absolutely.* Sometimes saying YES just simply means getting over ourselves, and instead of possessing self-confidence, we choose to say: I have God-confidence, Godfidence (It's a new word, y'all). We may not be qualified, but He sure is, and when we have Him, then YES we can do this!

I picked up a lot of tips on this leg of my journey. One, be sure to pray about where God wants you to go to church. The leadership you are under matters because they can either call you higher or hold you down. Two, if you are under healthy leaders, trust their judgment. Often, leadership can see things in you that you cannot yet see in yourself. When asked to step into a position of authority, always pray and ask God if this is Him opening the door or if it's a person's idea. If it is the Lord, even though you may feel unqualified, trust He will qualify you as you step out. Three, rely on the Holy Spirit to make up for any weaknesses. Let His wisdom flow through and bring fresh energy and ideas to you. Four, if the assignment is extra stretching, find scriptures to learn and speak out to renew your mind and give you courage. The Word of God is active and sharper than any two-edged sword (Hebrews 4:12).

> IT'S NOT OUR ABILITY GOD NEEDS; IT IS OUR AVAILABILITY.

Pray. Trust your leaders. Believe Jesus will help. Count on the Holy Spirit. Use the Word.

STRETCHING YOUR YES

SCRIPTURE TO APPLY:
But He said to me, "My grace is sufficient for you, for My power is perfected in weakness." Therefore I will boast all the more gladly in my weaknesses, so that the power of Christ may rest on me. 2 Corinthians 12:9 NIV

SONG TO LISTEN:
"Your Spirit," Tasha Cobbs Leonard

QUESTIONS:
In what ways do you find yourself leading? At home, work, church?

Have you ever let your lack of qualifications stop you from accepting a leadership position? Explain.

When have you experienced the tangible strength of Christ flowing through you for a task or situation?

Share about a time the Holy Spirit spoke through you or brought wisdom to you for a situation.

CHALLENGE:
Think of one thing in your life God has called you to in this season that feels hard or out of your element. Ask the Lord to specifically give you courage and grace for this situation. Write down one scripture and say it out loud to help you overcome any nervous feelings.

I'LL SAY YES
Even if...
I don't know how

Ummmm how am I going to do that? I wondered how to accomplish the suggested feat before me. I felt a persistent and gentle lead of the Holy Spirit to write a book, but I wasn't sure if I had the capacity, know-how, or education for such a task. Since I was unsure, I sought confirmation to affirm what I was feeling, which is something I always do when taking a big step of faith. I believe God is not only okay with us asking for a sign, but He welcomes it. Check out what Isaiah 7:11 says, "Ask the LORD your God for a sign, whether in the deepest depths or in the highest heights." I asked for a sign and I got it.

Within a week, three different sources mentioned I should write a book, which up until this point in my life, no one had ever done.

"I think it's time to write *your* book."

"You always recommend books, but I'm wondering when *you* are going to write one."

"I love these short devotions you share, so when is *your* book coming out?"

I had my confirmation, now for my message.

What topic should I write about, Father?

"Me."

What? No. I don't have the credentials for that.

"What credentials?"

Well you know, I'd like to point out the most obvious: I didn't go to college and most certainly didn't attend seminary, I'm not ordained or accredited, a theologian or evangelist. Like, I'm not your girl. I think you meant to tell someone else this.

"But are you my daughter?"

Yes… and?

"Write about me from a daughter's perspective. You've got a different point of view than your brothers."

This really resonated with me. I have a daughter and two sons, and I can testify firsthand that fathers interact with their girls a whole lot differently than their boys. Andrew and Emma have a unique daddy-daughter relationship. With our girl, my husband is more gentle, tender, and nurturing. With the boys, it's all play, rough and tough, and character building. Emma has a unique perspective of her dad, and to get the full picture of Andrew, you would need to hear not only Drew and Jack talk about him but hear from her as well. So I asked the kids separately how they would describe daddy. Note their responses.

Drew and Jack: Dad is fun, takes us places, and plays with us.
Emma: Dad is protective, kind, awesome, and handsome.

Even the simple answers of my kids illustrate the importance of hearing from both the sons and daughters of God to get the full picture. So the Holy Spirit's prompting to write from a daughter's perspective sealed the deal.

Just in case you haven't picked up the pattern, God ALWAYS has the best comebacks and I never win arguments with Him. While I may not have been credentialed on paper to write a book on the God of the universe, I most certainly could write about *my* Father, *my* Savior, *my* Holy Spirit. I said YES. Consequently, this is what the book is about, getting to know God as Father, God as Son, and God as Holy Spirit. The Lord gave me this beautiful picture of explaining what happens to a person who gets to know the triune God—not just Jesus, not just Yahweh, not just the Spirit—but learning about Him as a whole. He showed me a tree and reminded me that a seed has almost all it needs to become a tree, except it will need *good soil* (we must be rooted in the love of God the Father), the *right amount of sunlight* (we must be planted in the light of the Son, Jesus), and a *consistent water supply* (we must allow the living water of the Holy Spirit flow through us). We need to know all three persons of the trinity if we're to become those trees firmly planted by the streams of water, ever producing fruit (Psalms 1:3).

I said YES to writing *The Awesome One*, even though I had no training, had never taken writing classes, heck I didn't even know if I could write well. But I took on the challenge anyway—assuming by His track record, He'd equip me with the words needed to reach the people who needed to hear them. I said YES and trusted God with the rest!

> I SAID YES AND TRUSTED GOD WITH THE REST!

When the Holy Spirit asks us to do seemingly impossible tasks, we are given the invitation to face our own limitations. When we're up against improbable odds, it's essential to recount His faithfulness. How did He come through before? How did He provide? How did He make a way? How did He equip us? When we look back on our previous experiences, we are reminded that if God did it once, He can do it again, and again, and again.

At the time I began writing my first book, I didn't know *how*, but I did know *who*— who would show me the way. After committing to say YES, I sat down one day to write, prayed for the Holy Spirit to help, and the words just flowed like a river. The anointing fell. I wrote and I wrote and I wrote—it was all-consuming. When passion for a project wells up and overflows out of you, it can be easy to let it take over the other responsibilities in your life. I was becoming a writer, but I was also a daughter of God, a wife, a mother of small children, and a ministry leader. Even though I knew that getting these words onto paper was a Heavenly assignment, I still needed to learn how to balance it with the other hats I wore.

First, with all the "pouring out" I was doing, it was imperative to continually fill up. Time with God was not just something to check off the "good-Christian" list, it was my life source and still is to this day. For me, this always includes worship, and it can't just be background noise, I need to actually sing praises. Then, I open the Word and ask the Holy Spirit to teach me something new. My highlighter is always ready and my journal is always open to scribble down any verse that sticks out or any whispers I hear from Heaven. This time is about being with Jesus. In the Secret Place, I meet with God and He meets with me, and there is no other thing on this planet that satisfies and refreshes my soul like time with Him.

Second, I had to prioritize family. We came up with a schedule of times I would write and when I would spend time with my loved ones. My husband and I committed to a date night at least twice a month and which evenings we would watch our favorite shows together. Eating dinner together was and is a big deal to us. Going on family walks and Friday movie nights were a must. Those closest to me needed to know they were more important than what I was doing, and I found the breaks from the writing process actually fueled my creativity. Turns out, resting and taking your mind off a project to have fun supplies you with fresh ideas and inspiration! God wants us to live abundantly as we walk out our YES.

> GOD WANTS US TO LIVE ABUNDANTLY AS WE WALK OUT OUR YES.

It is amazing how God expands our capacity as we pray for strength and help to walk out our callings. I asked Him for wisdom and grace with each step of the journey in front of me, recognizing that no two people have the same path. We are not designed to live another person's life, just our own, which is why comparison is a dangerous trap. My gifts, capacities, and purposes are different from those around me, as they should be—my job was to stay within *my* circle of grace and trust God would stay with me with each new step I took.

Remember in the story of the Good Samaritan what the hero

does after he helps bind up the wounds?

He went over to him and bandaged his wounds, pouring on olive oil and wine. <u>Then he put him on his own animal, brought him to an inn, and took care of him.</u>

He led the injured to safety, guiding him the whole way. But that's not all! The man *continued* to care for him. This is what our Savior does for us on our journey. Jesus doesn't just point out the way to go, He takes us there. He did this for me throughout my writing journey, carefully guiding me along the way. God didn't lead me to write a book and say, "Well good luck!" No, He is faithful to travel with us on the path of our calling. When you imagine yourself walking toward a place God is leading, where is He taking you? God can be beside you, in front of you, sometimes behind you, or other times, He is carrying you the whole way. Remember that you are never walking alone.

The rough draft was completed in less than nine months, and it was the easiest book I ever wrote. But holding a finished manuscript isn't the same thing as having it published. I soon found out I still had a long way to go.

What now, God?

"Get it published."

How?

"I'll show you."

So I did what every Millennial does to become an overnight

expert, I typed in Google: "How to publish a book." I discovered there were lots of different options. After much research and deliberation, I decided to pursue the traditional publishing route, which meant I needed to get my manuscript picked up by a literary agency. Now, in order for this to happen, I would have to compile a killer book proposal (had no idea how!) AND write an outstanding query letter (didn't know what this was!). I ascertained this letter was the whole key to getting noticed. If an author's query letter wasn't a hit, then the agent would NEVER even read the book proposal… and I had no clue how to write one! Haha! Clearly, I was crushing it as I embarked on this publishing journey. Yeah, right.

Since I didn't know the first thing about query letters, I went back to my trusted study buddy, Google, and searched the pages of the World Wide Web to get all the best tips on writing this dynamic letter. I worked tirelessly over the next few months on the book proposal, query letter, and researching literary agents in my genre. Finally, I found a few agents who might be a good fit for my message. After my editor fixed the crap out of the initial query letter and proposal, I sent it out, along with all my hopes to become a published author and complete my YES to God.

"You actually got an answer back?!" My editor exclaimed in shock! *Obviously, she was a real big fan of my writing.* I'm only kidding, to explain her surprise, she had warned me that many first-time authors never hear back from agents. We were both blown away. Miracle number one.

Not only did an agent want to work with me, but he OWNED the agency! Another shocker! He was seasoned in the publishing industry and was willing to take a gamble on me, but he required me to make some changes in order to work with his agency. Miracle number two.

The first condition was, I essentially needed to get famous online. Haha! He explained how the industry had changed and publishers *used* to pick up writers with a great message and help grow their platform, but *now*, they required authors to have their own platform to secure a contract. This was not the news I wanted to receive and was disappointed to hear the industry had taken this turn. While I was willing to try this route if God wanted me to, I wrestled with deciding my next steps. Secondly, I must switch my audience from all Christians to just women. I did not have peace about this as I felt the message was for all of God's children, regardless of gender. Also, women are already familiar with the daughter perspective of God… I wanted this to be a resource for the sons too. I felt they needed to hear something about their Heavenly Father that we alone can reveal.

I said NO on both accounts. Not right away, of course, as I took those conditions to God in prayer, seeking wisdom by inquiring if this was what *He* required of me. I had been faithful throughout the writing process, and I could see that doors were being opened. No matter how much I wanted this book to be published, the requirement of "growing my followers" was not aligning with my values. Online fame is not a life goal of mine, and I sensed there was no need to change this in order to complete my YES. I trusted that if God wanted me to have a larger platform, He would help me grow it organically. God had asked me to write a book, not grow a following.

I was reminded of King David, who had NO followers or anyone who believed in Him when he hit the battle scene and stepped out to slay Goliath… only God. Although I understood the risk, if King David could accomplish what God asked him to do with only a sling and five stones, I could say YES without a platform. With full trust that God would show me the way to publish the book, I contacted the agent and respectfully declined the offer.

I spent months working towards this publishing route, and wondered why God had led me down this path—had it been a waste of time? Even though I trusted Him, I was confused. So, what were my other options? I could pay-to-publish with an Indie publisher or self-publish. The latter was definitely out of the question because I didn't know a thing about that. So I looked at independent publishing options and they were not cheap. It was easy to find a publisher who'd work with me, for an outrageous amount of money. *How are people supposed to get Kingdom messages out if they're not rich or famous, God?!* Back to the drawing board.

After months of researching, hitting roadblocks and detours, I found my answer: I *would* self-publish my book, though I lacked the know-how. If God got me this far I was confident He'd get me across the finish line, so back to good ole' Google I went. And after much trial and error, blood, sweat, and tears, plus a little spiritual warfare mixed in there—I accomplished one of the hardest tasks of my life.

It's ACTUALLY here! Phew! I never want to do that again, was all I could think when I finally held my very own book in my hands. The journey was hard, but God was faithful. I said YES, and He showed me the way.

Isn't it funny how sometimes the road we absolutely, under no

> Y'ALL, SOMETIMES OUR WAY ISN'T RIGHT! BUT YOU KNOW WHO'S WAY IS? GOD'S, EVERY TIME.

circumstances want to take ends up being the very path our feet tread upon? Even though we may think it's not the best route, God knows our future, He knows the roads we must walk to prepare us for our destiny. This is why we must "Lean not on our own understanding, in all our ways acknowledge Him and He will make our path straight" (Proverbs 3:5-6). AND we must not demand "our own way." Y'all, sometimes our way isn't right! But you know who's way is? God's, every time. And where He guides He provides—resources, finances, know-how, all of it. He's just looking for our YES.

Purpose found in our YES

So our pain does have a greater purpose. This story did not end when my book was published. It was only the beginning. A few months later, my life changed while sitting in a business meeting with my husband. The speaker shared her dream of using the pain from her past to help others overcome their wounds—to open a rehabilitation center for women coming out of human trafficking for them to learn life skills and how to function in society again. Wow. What a noble dream! Do you know what my dream board consisted of at the time? A nice farmhouse, a couple of vacation homes, and a white Jeep Wrangler. After I sat in the meeting, all I could think of was the scene from the Disney movie *Tangled* where Rapunzel shares her dream and it's beautiful and purposeful. Then, the selfish Flynn Rider shares his self-serving dream and someone bluntly informs him: Your dream stinks. Guys, my dream stunk! It was all about me. It served me. It helped no one.

As fast as I could run to the secret place—what I affectionately call the space where I have my quiet time—I asked my Father for a new dream. Had I walked through anything painful that possibly played a part in my calling? I did not have a bad childhood or face any major trauma, for which I'm grateful. I couldn't think of any wound that would fuel my purpose.

What's my purpose, God? What am I even supposed to do?

That's when the Holy Spirit whispered something back.

"What difficulty have you walked through this past year?"

What? Publishing? Oh heck yeah, that's hard! To be an "uninfluential" (by the world's standards) Christian writer not rolling in the dough; It. Was. Hard.

And the next phrase changed my life and just might change yours:

"Well, what are you going to do about it?"

Instantly, I knew.

I'm going to start a publishing company!

In a split-second, I said *YES, let's do this!* From this moment on, I began dreaming big with God. I didn't hesitate on this one. I did not push back because I wasn't qualified. I said YES because I knew my God was calling, and I knew my God was faithful! He would give me the know-how, steps to take, and people to help. If this was a Kingdom mission, He'd bring me Kingdom resources, and He has!

We created United House Publishing, a company that is fun, inexpensive, and has no "platform" requirements—making publishing a book attainable, affordable, and enjoyable. Basically making sure the authors had what I did not. As soon as I said YES, the creativity exploded. When there was a need for it, He released it. Ideas flooded my mind constantly, and I knew they were Heaven inspired because they were unlike anything I'd ever done before, some, no one had! I want to just hover here for a second. I had zero creative publishing ideas *until* I stepped out. I'm convinced God has this reservoir of Kingdom creativity, and as soon as He spots someone who is willing to dream big with Him, He turns the dial and releases a river of Heavenly ingenuity and inspiration.

Every time I needed something, we prayed as a team and God provided! If it was resources, they came. If it was a new teammate, they showed up. If it was a skill set, we learned. Remember all those other publishing paths I researched and attempted? I learned the best parts of each route and put it ALL into United House Publishing. Even the pain I felt having to jump through all the hoops, take the steps to get "noticed," and feeling poor because I couldn't afford the pay-to-publish fees, it fueled my passion to make the system better, to make it look like the Kingdom—God doesn't look at any of those things. He notices and values the overlooked and the poor. I was guided down this difficult path for a reason. I am here to tell you the Lord is faithful. Saying a YES is our job, making a way is His!

HE CAN DO ANYTHING WITH ANYONE HE WANTS.

So if I can tell you anything from this

YES, it's that God does not need your credentials or degrees. Will He use them? Yes! But He doesn't need them, and I for one am glad because I had neither! He can do ANYTHING with ANYONE He wants. If we have the Holy Spirit living within us, then we have the strength of God coursing through our veins enabling us to walk out the calling on our lives. By ourselves, we're not able! We're not enough. We're incapable of wearing all the hats and doing all the things. But with God we are able!

A few things to take away from my book writing journey and opening a Kingdom company are: First, say YES even if you don't quite know how to do it yet! God can and will show you. Second, always, always, always ask Him about the right path. If you don't like His answer… TRUST HIM ANYWAY! While it might be more difficult, there's purpose in it.

Third, when you're unsure of the outcome, recount the ways God has been faithful to you in the past. Recalling the ways He provided and came through in the past builds your faith. Fourth, when praying about your purpose (which can shift seasonally), consider the pain points in your life. How can you help others heal? Say YES and see God use you in ways you never thought possible!!!

Say YES without the know-how. Trust God on the journey. Recount His faithfulness. Look for purpose from pain.

STRETCHING YOUR YES

SCRIPTURE TO APPLY:
I pray that from his glorious, unlimited resources he will empower you with inner strength through his Spirit. Ephesians 3:16

SONG TO LISTEN:
"Faithful Now," Vertical Worship

QUESTIONS:
Do you feel a stirring to do something but don't think you're equipped for the task?

Have you ever recalled God's faithfulness to encourage you to trust Him again?

What part of the story can encourage you to pursue this nudge from the Holy Spirit?

Tell about a time you were asked to do something beyond your capacity, but God supplied you with supernatural strength and know-how to complete it.

CHALLENGE:
Grab a journal and sneak away to the secret place. Now, ask the Holy Spirit to reveal any difficult or painful experience that may play a part of your purpose. None of our pain points are in vain. Pray and ask God if He wants to birth anything from your past difficulties and share the answer with a trusted friend.

8

I'LL SAY YES
Even if...
It's not in my plan

Are you sure that was God? I inquired skeptically when Andrew called and enthusiastically announced, "I think we're supposed to move to North Carolina!" What?! This was NOT a part of my plan at all. And I did not welcome or want this interruption to my perfectly mapped out life.

We had just wrapped up renovations on our beautiful house—gutting it back to the studs—complete Fixer Upper style. I got to pick out everything, and it was a dream come true. It was located in the most charming small downtown, where I could walk, yes walk, to a quaint, craft coffee shop. A picturesque park waited across the street from our home to provide hours of fun for our kiddos, and we often sat on our hill overlooking high school students posing for prom and homecoming pictures at *the spot* in town to take photos. We loved where we lived.

Andrew's career as a General Contractor was going wonderfully, working alongside his dad for twenty years. The company was growing, innovating, and going well. It was steady, predictable, and a blessing. He loved his job.

Our church was AMAZING. Our faith community was everything we ever dreamed of being a part of. We were accepted and empowered, challenged to grow, and felt included and wanted. Our small group ministry was flourishing, and we enjoyed belonging to a healthy ministry that was reaching our community. You don't find a church family like this every day. We loved our church.

We were surrounded by family, had an incredible group of friends, and entertained all the time. The local schools were fabulous, we either biked or walked the kids every day (when the streets weren't snow-covered, obv.). Basically, we LOVED our lives, if you haven't picked that up already. Sooooo while I always say YES to God, I needed to know this was a God idea before I could commit. Surprisingly, I partially already felt like it was because I'd never choose to leave all this. Often, when it goes against what your flesh wants, it could be a sure sign it is what God wants.

Any ideas as to how I made sure God was leading us to NC? Did you guess, "You asked for confirmation?" Ding ding ding, correct! In my quiet time the next day, I inquired of the Lord.

Alright God this is uncomfortable and I need to know this is Your idea, not ours. I thought we'd be here forever. Please confirm in a big way if we're supposed to leave all this and move to North Carolina.

"Don't you want to go on an adventure with me?" He replied.

What, of course! I'm always up for adventures with You... if I know it's You.

"You must go to North Carolina because <u>there is freedom for you there</u>."

Hmmmmm. I took out my journal and wrote down what I believed God whispered to me in this sacred moment. As I began to pray, it hit me: if we moved to North Carolina, I knew exactly where we would go to church; a ministry we had learned from for years. Their small group pastor had poured into us, they hosted and trained us, allowing Andrew and me to shadow their staff for a weekend, and we never missed their Christmas and New Year's service. *God, are we supposed to attend that church?!*

As I live and breathe, in that very moment, I "internally" asked God that question. The YouTube video which had been playing a kids program on my TV suddenly switched to playing a message by the pastor of that very church, and, as if this wasn't enough, the pastor made a bold statement, "You can't camp out where God has called you to pass through."

I could have stayed in Michigan my whole life. I had set up camp and never planned to leave, but I was beginning to sense God was calling us to pass through. Saying YES to God is also a lifestyle of surrender. It means not our plans but His be done.

As if this wasn't enough confirmation, He did more. As I continued my quiet time that morning, I picked up the book *Captivating* by John and Stasi Eldredge, and two statements sealed the deal:

"The invitations of our Prince come to us in all sorts of ways… An invitation delivered in the most intimate and personalized way… <u>it is a call to adventure.</u>"[2]

"God really does want you to know who *you* are. He wants you to be able to understand the story of your life, to know where you have come from, and to know where you are going. <u>There is freedom there.</u>"³

Adventure. Freedom. The EXACT two things the Holy Spirit said to me and I had scribbled in my journal. I burst into tears, not only because I heard His voice clearly but because He was answering my prayer right before my eyes, instantaneously. I jumped on the phone and through my tears choked out the words, "We *are* supposed to move to North Carolina."

We had our heading AND we had our confirmation.

Our plan was to work for the family business and raise our kids at our beloved church in Michigan; God had another. While we loved our life there, we were committed to: "Where you go, I go. Where you lead, I follow." A life of saying YES is a commitment to going where and when He leads. If He calls, we just answer… not for fear of punishment or being "out of His will," but because we don't want to miss out on an adventure with the God of the universe. This is why. I'll be darned if I let someone else get to live the adventures I was supposed to have with God because I said NO. I will have them ALL!

I gotta jump back to my boy, the Good Samaritan, here. Keeping in mind he was on a journey, do you think he figured into his travel plans stopping to help someone, therefore delaying his trip by at least a day?

But a Samaritan <u>on his journey</u> came up to him, and when he saw the man, he had compassion. He went over to him and bandaged his wounds, pouring on olive oil and wine. Then he put him on his own animal, brought him to an inn, and took care of him. *The next day* he took out two denarii, gave them to the innkeeper, and said, 'Take care of him. When I come back I'll reimburse you for whatever extra you spend.'

I'm going to go out on a limb here and assume the Samaritan probably didn't plan on saving someone's life or postponing his journey that day, but according to the story, his compassion prompted him to throw his plans out the window. He chose to be a neighbor when no one else would because he welcomed interruptions. Since we are determined to live our lives this way, then, like the Samaritan, when God calls, we must go. We must be willing to sacrifice our agenda for His. Saying YES to God requires flexibility.

> SAYING YES TO GOD REQUIRES FLEXIBILITY.

Saying YES tests our Faith

So saying yes isn't always a walk in the park. Once I had my confirmation, it wasn't instantly sunshine and rainbows. I struggled to leave my home, family, and friends… and in my quiet time one day, God gave me something precious to cling to. I found a promise I'd never paid much attention to:

Peter began to tell him, "Look, we have left everything and followed you."

"Truly I tell you," Jesus said, "there is no one who has left house or brothers or sisters or mother or father or children or fields for my sake and for the sake of the gospel, who will not receive a hundred times more, now at this time—houses, brothers and sisters, mothers and children, and fields, with persecutions—and eternal life in the age to come. But many who are first will

be last, and the last first. Mark 10:28-31 CSB

How's He going to lead me here? How's this passage going to specifically mention a "house," family, brothers, and sisters, and promise to restore that, "now, at this time"? Only God, y'all. He's so faithful. This was the exact word I needed to get me through the difficult but God-inspired move.

Saying YES isn't always easy, but He never promised a smooth ride, just to be with and see us through. If you find yourself in a difficult YES, ask your good, good Father to send a word of hope. Ask Him to show you a promise to hold on to.

> NEVER AGREE WITH THOSE WHO DON'T BELIEVE FOR THE MIRACULOUS.

Saying YES was the first step but selling our house in a buyers market was next. We calculated a specific number we needed, and I'll just go ahead and tell you it was going to take a miracle to get this. It would be the highest a home had sold in our neighborhood in years. We had a few naysayers say we'd never get it, but our anthem became: God can do it! Never agree with those who don't believe for the miraculous. When God has spoken something to us, we do not let the skeptical words of others derail our hope. We take their words captive right away and remind them (respectfully) or ourselves what God is able to do. The way to stop the Enemy from planting a seed of doubt is to root it out right away!

The first appraisal came in… $100,000 LESS than we needed. After hardly any showings, and an estimated value way lower than we expected, we took our situation to God and said, *Lord, You know what we need, we know with You ALL things are possible. You called us to North Carolina, we need You to make a way— like only You can.*

We had heard the call, but the waters standing between us and our promised land had not parted yet. The way hadn't been cleared. But we knew *without a doubt* He was sending us to North Carolina, and He would get us there, so we chose to make a bold move. After praying and asking God about the timing of when we should start the moving process, we both felt He said "now."

Now? Now, before you make a way? Now, before we have money from a house sale? You want us to go now?!

After hearing clearly and seeking the wisdom from our pastors, we decided to not only believe God could make a way but show Him we trusted His every word by stepping out in faith. The kids and I packed up and headed to our "promised land" *before* the house sold! We went down to scope out the land and report back to Andrew what we could find. We would not have made this move without seeking God and trusted advisers on the timing of the word He'd spoken. Sometimes promises take a while to come to fruition, but we stepped since we knew without a shadow of a doubt He had said "now." When making big decisions always, always, always consider the timing of God and seek His and other wise counsel.

Sometimes on your YES journey, God will pull a "Moses" on you. He'll part the sea, making the situation and next steps crystal clear so you can have confidence for your journey. I like the Moses way. It's easy and requires less faith because you can see the way. But sometimes, He calls you to be a "Joshua," where He tells you to go and declares He'll stop the flow of water, making the journey and next steps clearer AS you step out in faith. In the book of Joshua, when the Israelietes approached the river separating them from their promised land, the water was still flowing... but because the Lord essentially said, "Step out and then I'll make a way," the priests of Israel plunged their feet into the overflowing waters of the Jordan River, and what happened?

It was the harvest season, and the Jordan was overflowing its banks. But as soon as the feet of the priests who were carrying the Ark touched the water at the river's edge, the water above that point began backing up a great distance away at a town called Adam, which is near Zarethan. And the water below that point flowed on to the Dead Sea until the riverbed was dry. Then all the people crossed over near the town of Jericho.
Joshua 3:15-16

As soon as their feet touched the river, as soon as they stepped out on the word from the Lord, the waters parted. *Come on now!* This story was my guide. In faith, we took the only step we knew how and guess what happened?! Once we took a giant leap across the Mason Dixon line, a family toured our house and loved it. *After* I left, not *before*. They were willing to pay higher, but the appraisal had to reflect the price we were asking. We needed a miracle! So we asked the Miracle Worker to move, and guess what? Another company came in and appraised our property at $100,000 higher than the last! I don't think I need to tell you that it's not *common* to have that big of a difference in appraisals within a month. But we serve the God of the *uncommon*, the God of the impossible, and He worked a miracle. We stepped out in faith, and He showed Himself faithful!

While saying YES is full of adventures and you get to see God show up in big ways, it does come at the cost of no longer sitting in the driver's seat in the car of life. It's a choice to literally say,

"Jesus, take the wheel," and mean it. It's great. It's exciting, but sometimes it means giving up something you love, because of the One you love.

This YES taught me His plans aren't necessarily my plans, but when I stop making life about me and what I want, I might just witness God do some pretty cool miracles. I may get to see things others don't because I'm willing to do what others won't. I also learned sometimes we need to move on a YES before anything has shifted—as a matter of fact, things may not change until we step out. Lastly, it taught me the importance of seeking God on the timing of His promise. Sometimes He gives us a word, but if we're not aware of God's timeline for this promise, we may try to step out but until it's the right time, it won't happen. Our faith doesn't force His hand but instead works with Him—following as He leads in His perfect timing.

> SOMETIMES IT MEANS GIVING UP SOMETHING YOU LOVE, BECAUSE OF THE ONE YOU LOVE.

The tips I acquired on this YES adventure were many. First, I recommend pre-surrendering your plans to God. What I mean is predetermine that you will allow Him to interrupt your agenda and consider what He asks of you. A life of saying YES is one filled with mystery because you don't really know where it is going to lead. Second, ask for all the confirmation you need. It has been my experience that the Lord *wants* to confirm His plan for you. Third, when the "ask" is life-changing, seek godly counsel!! This can be your pastor, but it could also be a friend or family member you trust and is deeply connected with God. Don't just ask people who will tell you what you want to hear, ask those who will say what you need to hear. Fourth, guard your heart against skeptical naysayers. They come in every form and can be Christians or non-believers. Know what God said, and reject anything that doesn't align with His word. This protects your seed from being stolen. Fifth, you may have to take a leap of faith before all your ducks are in a row. If the Holy Spirit is leading, be willing to step out in faith, trusting Him to guide and make the way.

Allow God's interruptions. Get confirmation. Seek wise counsel. Protect your heart. Step out in faith.

STRETCHING YOUR YES

SCRIPTURE TO APPLY:
The wind blows where it pleases, and you hear its sound, but you don't know where it comes from or where it is going. So it is with everyone born of the Spirit.
John 3:8 CSB

SONG TO LISTEN:
"Over and Over," Vertical Worship

QUESTIONS:
Has God ever unexpectedly changed your plan? When?

How willing are you to allow the Holy Spirit to interrupt your agenda?

Is there a situation you are facing where the Lord is asking you to step out before the way is clear?

Share an example of a time you took a leap of faith and how God showed up and did something miraculous.

CHALLENGE:
Practice allowing Holy Spirit interruptions. How do you do that? Say a prayer to God the Father, giving Him permission to change up your agenda for the day if He has another plan. And then, when something unexpected pops up, don't get stressed, but instead pray and ask God how you can partner with the Holy Spirit in that moment.

9

I'LL SAY YES
Even if...
I don't think I'm the one for the job

What could I tell them? When the Holy Spirit put volunteering at a local women's rehab center on my heart, I wasn't sure I was "the girl for the job." I was going about my life serving at church and attending a Bible study—nothing too out of the ordinary—but at study one night, a friend made an extraordinary statement that forever changed me.

"I got off work early one day this week, so I seized the opportunity to go help out a local non-profit." It shocked me to hear she took the initiative to do this on her own. She didn't wait for a church "serve day" or sign-up sheet. She researched local ministries and non-profits that had a need, and my friend Natalie used her skills and time to meet those needs.

Honestly, I had NEVER experienced someone like this, and I certainly never volunteered outside of church. Her example pricked my heart.

Then, the call of God beckoned to stretch me once again.

"I want you to go lead a Bible study at Dove's Nest."

I'LL SAY YES

What? No. They probably don't let just anybody come to lead a study.

"I want you to lead a Bible study there."

Mmmmmmm... I'm not sure.

Dove's Nest is Charlotte Rescue Mission's facility for women recovering from addiction— and my hesitation stemmed from my inexperience. After this back and forth, the conversation went quiet, but the feeling would not go away. I considered calling the organization and inquiring, but I never did. I thought about it on and off for months. I kept praying to verify I "heard correctly." Ever do that? Ever think you heard God but aren't quite sure if it was His idea or yours? You're not alone.

I soon discovered it was 100% the voice of the Holy Spirit pulling me. Serving at a new members' class, I introduced myself to an unfamiliar face, "Hey! I'm Amber, are you new here?"

"Um, no I've been attending for a while." The lady responded slightly confused, as was I— trying to piece together what she was doing in this particular class, if she wasn't new.

"Well, I'm the new one here so that could be why we haven't met yet," I fumbled to recover from the potentially awkward situation.

"I've been hit or miss the past few months, but I'm attending this meeting because I'm the church's liaison for Dove's Nest. I coordinate the people from church with the volunteer opportunities at our org."

All I could think was: *Are ya now?* It became apparent to me that this was a divine connection, and while I was hesitating to say YES, God brought the opportunity right to my lap.

"Funny that you say that… you see, I've had this burning desire for months to lead a Bible study at Dove's Nest—do you guys even allow something like that?"

Her face lit up in amazement and, in complete shock, exclaimed, "Are you kidding me right now?! About six months ago, our pastor's wife came and shared the gospel with the women and has wanted someone to lead a Bible study there ever since. We haven't been able to find anyone who would commit. She's literally been praying for someone to rise up and do this!"

I was undone. The whole time I had been feeling the tug to come and lead a Bible study, someone else was praying a person would rise up for this very assignment. Look at God! His faithfulness is unmatched. Even though I wavered in walking out this YES, He never did. He was making a very obvious way for me to get there.

My new friend spoke to the director and quickly got a Bible study on the schedule. On my end, I was praying for a team of women to help me lead the ladies, and God assembled a passionate, anointed group. We chose the material, made a plan, advertised for an upcoming Bible study with free coffee (we are not above bribing with caffeine if it gets people to Jesus—whatever it takes!), and we PRAYED. We hoped a few women would show up.

Then, the first day of our study arrived, and with it, came doubt.

Lord, you made it crystal clear that I'm called to do this and opened every

I'll SAY YES

door, but what am I going to say to these women? They've seen stuff I have not. I don't have experience here, I'm just a little, white, Christian girl. I am seriously not trained for this.

"I am with you, and I will help you. Go. I will show up."

I trusted Him more than I trusted myself. And I went. I pushed past my insecurities and inexperience and gave God my YES and my presence and relied on Him in me to do the work.

We arrived early and set up a few chairs, hoping half would be filled that morning. Our team was willing to start small. We planned on a tiny intimate group as we set up those chairs that Saturday, knowing if only one lady showed up, it would be worth it.

We waited in anticipation to see if anyone would come, and the ladies started trickling in. One, two, three… and on and on. Guys, so many women poured in that we had to get more chairs!! Half of the residents attended! Either they wanted free coffee or they wanted to grow closer to God, and we didn't care which it was, we were just happy they came! We had not expected this. God likes to exceed our expectations.

As we stood up to lead, some of the women were definitely guarded… I could not read them and wondered if they'd like me at all. So I prayed for courage, asking God to speak through me, and I told myself: *Pretend they all like you. Be yourself and talk to them as if they love you.*

You know the great thing about being genuine? It's easy to keep up. Pretending to be someone you are not is exhausting. Ain't

Even if... I don't think I'm the one for the job

nobody got time for it. Everyone leading the study was completely themselves. I even voiced what I felt some may be thinking:

"I know you may be thinking: 'What's this white little church girl going to tell me?' But ya know what, we're here because God sent us to tell you He loves you and show you He cares." The honesty broke the room and unlocked the women.

YOU KNOW THE GREAT THING ABOUT BEING GENUINE? IT'S EASY TO KEEP UP.

Our entire team of ladies brought their strengths and experience with a loving God to the table, and the Bible study became like nothing I'd ever witnessed. My friend Angela had worked in inner-city schools and she "handled her business" leading with her passion for Jesus and shutting down tangents if needed—as only she could. Stacey led with feistiness, and she taught the women the secrets of silencing lies by shanking the Devil and replacing them with the truth of the Word. Natalie led in kindness, with compassion and faithfulness—her heartfelt words of wisdom were often accompanied by tears. It was a dream team, all of us discovering the courage we didn't know we had.

In the story of the Good Samaritan, it doesn't say he ran to the local store to grab supplies or was trained in administering first aid but instead used the resources and know-how he possessed.

But a Samaritan on his journey came up to him, and when he saw the man, he had compassion. <u>He went over to him and bandaged his wounds, pouring on olive oil and wine. Then he put him on his own animal</u>, brought him to an inn, and took care of him.

Even though it doesn't say he was a doctor, the Samaritan poured in wine and oil, then bandaged the victim. The story didn't mention he was professionally trained to heal wounds, it just said he was available and used what know-how and resources he had to help. When God presents us with a big, out-of-our-element opportunity, we can either declare: "I'm not the one for the job, I have no professional training in this! I can't help," or we can say, "Okay, I might not know it all, but I know a little and, most importantly, I know You. I'll use what I have and rely on You, God, to make up the difference." While the Good Samaritan may have deviated from his original plan, he used his compassion, experience, and resources to help heal someone else! And potentially saved their life. With God, we can do this, too.

The Urgency of our YES

So a sense of urgency can catapult your witness. At Dove's Nest, we occasionally gave an invitation to know Jesus as Savior, and women started choosing to follow Christ! It was what Christians dream of seeing, and God let us be a part of it. When you say YES to God, I can promise your Christian walk won't be boring. It became so exciting to see what God would do each week at group.

Then out of nowhere, tragedy hit. One of the ladies had left the facility and she took her last breath when she overdosed. This was someone in our Bible study, we saw her every week, and we were all devastated. At first, we started blaming ourselves like we hadn't done enough, but then God reminded us of her coming forward to accept Jesus at group. What if my team and I had never been there? What if we said NO? But we didn't say no, we listened to God, and we got to spend her last weeks on earth

Even if... I don't think I'm the one for the job

together. I believe we'll see her in Heaven! Experiencing this death changed things for us... we were determined to invite women into a relationship with Jesus EVERY week. We didn't know if we'd see all our ladies the following week; some were graduating or leaving the program, so we didn't have time to waste. We felt

> WHEN YOU SAY YES TO GOD, I CAN PROMISE YOUR CHRISTIAN WALK WON'T BE BORING.

a sense of urgency that it was a "now or never" situation. Each week, we offered the salvation of Christ and to be filled with the Spirit, and each week, they responded! Transformation unfolded before our very eyes.

The ladies wanted to take the next step and get baptized. Because of the nature of this non-profit, it wasn't safe for all of the women to go in public or have photos taken, and while they rotated taking turns going in small groups to go to church, they didn't have the ability to transport a large group for baptisms. So we started praying for God to make a way. And don't you know, He did?! Our church heard about what was happening at our Bible study and they agreed to bring a baptismal tank to the facility to accommodate the large response from women!! This had never been done before at this org! Only God.

The day came! We had a beautiful, intimate ceremony set up in the outdoor courtyard, surrounded by a rose garden. Our lead pastor and his wife (whose prayers and faithfulness seeded this Bible study) came and encouraged the women. Then, to our surprise, the pastor who authored the Bible study we were using, climbed in the tank to baptize the women himself! It was so special. Over forty ladies lined up to declare their new life in Christ, including one of our co-leaders, and my best friend, Stacey! She joined the women and declared she was leaving the lies and anxiety of her past and stepping into her new righteous identity in Christ. It was unbelievable.

We led Bible study at Dove's Nest until the Covid-19 pandemic hit and they no longer permitted volunteers in the facility. Originally, our church had a hard time finding someone to commit to leading a study for twelve weeks, meanwhile, God graced us for eighteen months! Haha. Won't He do it?!

Do you think I would have said YES to step into a facility where some residents were there instead of serving prison time, some had been rescued out of trafficking, and most were recovering from alcohol and/or drug addiction—when I had no experience with any of this—if I had not been trained to say YES to the little things and witnessed God's faithfulness all along my journey? No way! All the little yeses lead to this big, way over my head YES!

This YES taught me the importance of being faithful in the small, behind-the-scenes opportunities so we may be entrusted with more. It also taught me that while we may not be experienced with certain issues or people groups, God is. If He's in us, then we literally have all we need. Jesus knows what strengths and personalities will minister to others. If God picks us for a task, there is a reason. We may doubt ourselves, but we can't doubt God, He knows what He's doing. Remember, it's about willingness, not experience!

This YES also taught me the brevity of life. We aren't guaranteed to see someone one more day—don't waste a moment. If you have an opportunity to tell someone about the love of God and how Jesus came to make a way for them to be in a relationship with the Father, ask them if they want to trust Jesus as Savior *now*. This is not a license to be pushy but, as the Spirit leads, give the option for people to choose and always be available to talk with them, lead them to the Lord, and allow them to ask questions—keeping in mind it's okay to say: "I don't know." The point is, we can't assume we'll have another chance, as I learned.

IF GOD PICKS US FOR A TASK, THERE IS A REASON.

My time at Dove's Nest left me with a pocket full of tips. First, you absolutely do not need training to make a difference in someone's life; you just need to be present. Will God use your life experiences to help others? Absolutely! But if you don't have those to bank on, trust God has what you need and say YES anyway. Don't let it stop you! Second, when the Holy Spirit puts something on your heart, and you don't know if it's possible—remember, you literally serve the God of the impossible, He can and will make a way for His plans, and He'll get you to what He has prepared for you! As long as our ship is moving, He'll steer it—it's easier to redirect a moving ship than a docked one.

Third, if you feel like you're not the one for the job, even if you don't trust yourself, trust the Lord. Be confident in His ability! Sure, maybe you feel ill-equipped, but this is the perfect opportunity for God's power to flow through you. Fourth, there is no time like now to invite people into a relationship with Jesus. Don't wait. Pray that God fills your heart with a sense of urgency for the lost. You don't have to be a trained evangelist to lead people to the Lord, just extend them an invitation!

Be present. God will make a way. Trust in the Lord's ability. Get them to Jesus, now!

I'LL SAY YES

STRETCHING YOUR YES

SCRIPTURE TO APPLY:
For all who are led by the Spirit of God are children of God. Romans 8:14

SONG TO LISTEN:
"Spirit Lead Me," Influence Music

QUESTIONS:
When have you felt like "you're not the one for the job"?

If the Holy Spirit leads you into unfamiliar waters, are you willing to follow?

Would you say your Christian walk is exciting or boring?

Share whether or not you feel a sense of urgency to lead others to Jesus. Share why or why not.

CHALLENGE:
The next time the Holy Spirit has a big ask of you, and you think "I'm not the one for the job," commit to saying YES anyway. Don't focus on your training or resources, look at God's. Is there something even now you feel stirred to do? If the timing is right, and the Spirit is leading, step out! Trust your Jehovah Jireh to provide everything and everyone you need to accomplish this huge assignment!

STARTING SMALL

On my adventure of getting to know the Holy Spirit, I learned if I was available and willing to be interrupted, I got to see God move in ways I'd only ever read about. Each YES displayed a "little" more of His character, heart, and power. Little things often get overlooked, but all those "littles" add up to a lot. The Lord no longer felt distant, as religion often implies. He was close and His Kingdom was here and now, ever-expanding. According to the world's standards, the bigger the better, but God flips everything in His Kingdom and makes a way for the small, the few, and the least to be important.

Parables of the Mustard Seed

Here is another illustration Jesus used: "The Kingdom of Heaven is like a mustard seed planted in a field. It is the smallest of all seeds, but it becomes the largest of garden plants; it grows into a tree, and birds come and make nests in its branches." Matthew 13:31-32

Jesus told them. "I tell you the truth, if you had faith even as small as a mustard seed, you could say to this mountain, 'Move from here to there,' and it would move. Nothing would be impossible." Matthew 17:20

Parable of the Yeast

Jesus also used this illustration: "The Kingdom of Heaven is like the yeast a woman used in making bread. Even though she put only a little yeast in three measures of flour, it permeated every part of the dough." Matthew 13:33

Jesus feeds 5,000

Jesus soon saw a huge crowd of people coming to look for him. Turning to

Philip, he asked, "Where can we buy bread to feed all these people?" He was testing Philip, for he already knew what he was going to do.

Philip replied, "Even if we worked for months, we wouldn't have enough money to feed them!"

Then Andrew, Simon Peter's brother, spoke up. "There's a young boy here with five barley loaves and two fish. But what good is that with this huge crowd?"

"Tell everyone to sit down," Jesus said. So they all sat down on the grassy slopes. (The men alone numbered about 5,000.) Then Jesus took the loaves, gave thanks to God, and distributed them to the people. Afterward he did the same with the fish. And they all ate as much as they wanted. John 6:5-11

The parable of the lost sheep

If a man has a hundred sheep and one of them wanders away, what will he do? Won't he leave the ninety-nine others on the hills and go out to search for the one that is lost? And if he finds it, I tell you the truth, he will rejoice over it more than over the ninety-nine that didn't wander away! In the same way, it is not my heavenly Father's will that even one of these little ones should perish. Matthew 18:12-14

Notice what each story has in common? The hidden value of something small. A minuscule mustard seed, a tiny amount of yeast, a few lunch box items, and one lost sheep. I used to place a lot of value on numbers; many still do, but these stories helped me "not despise the day of small beginnings" (Zec 4:10). Don't you just love our God? He came to shake up a broken system that screamed: numbers matter! When we give our YES to the Lord, it must come with a willingness to see and do things His way. Are we willing to both value and start small?

I'll Say Yes

Even if...
I have no training for this

I literally have no idea where to begin. When Andrew and I began sensing we needed to start a nonprofit ministry, we were both puzzled. *How? With who? What do we even do?* We had ALL the questions and didn't know where to find answers. We started praying for direction, and shortly after, we received a postcard in the mail from a lawyer who specialized in opening nonprofits. *Okay, God, we see you!* We said YES, even though we didn't know what we were doing. We reached out, and in less than three months, we opened United House Ministries with zero hiccups. Considering the hoops 501c3s have to jump through, we could not believe how quickly God moved the process along for us! He brought everything we needed right to our doorstep.

We started brainstorming and praying about what God wanted our ministry to look like and who we should ask to join us. Unity. Unity. Unity was consuming us. In the last prayer of Jesus, as He pours out His heart declared to the Father:

I have given them the glory you gave me, so they may be one as we are one. I am in them and you are in me. May they experience such perfect unity that the world will know that you sent me and that you love them as much as you

I'LL SAY YES

love me. John 17:22-23

If unity in the church results in the earth-shattering revelation that Jesus is the Messiah sent from God, then this would be the determined focus of our ministry.

We prayed about who to ask to be involved and invited everyone to our house to cast the vision. After sharing our hearts, each and every person said YES. Everyone was all in! We couldn't believe it! We were a grass-roots group of people who just loved God. Did we have a bunch of ministry training? Hardly. Were we sold out for Jesus? Absolutely. Though we didn't have much, we gave God what we had, like the little boy who offered his lunch to help feed a crowd.

There's a young boy here with five barley loaves and two fish. But what good is that with this huge crowd?"

"Tell everyone to sit down," Jesus said. So they all sat down on the grassy slopes. (The men alone numbered about 5,000.) Then Jesus took the loaves, gave thanks to God, and distributed them to the people. Afterward he did the same with the fish. And they all ate as much as they wanted.

> OUR "SMALL" IN THE HANDS OF GOD CAN BE MULTIPLIED.

Like the young boy, we didn't have much, but we took our "little" experience and offered it to our King. Our "small" in the hands of God can be multiplied and it was. Over the next year, we formed a family and hosted Freedom Nights. The music was powerful, I mean people were getting saved during praise and worship—before any message or invitation was given! We had a diverse group of speakers, male and female, from different ethnicities. Our prayer team prayed for miracles in the lives of those who came forward. We started hearing stories of breakthroughs, salvation, people healed of cancer, set free from a debilitating addiction, healing from infertility, homeless people miraculously finding homes, and we only met every few months. The response was, well, Kingdom.

We were gathering from all different denominations, genders, and ethnicities in one accord to glorify Jesus and the Lord commanded the blessing. We each came with our strength, our piece of the puzzle, and when combined, created a beautiful image. Then, the 2020 pandemic hit, and we had to cancel our events for a long time. Some of our team moved, went on to become community pastors and youth pastors, some went to the missions field, while others started their own ministry—everyone flourished. We felt we had been a loving community who allowed people to blossom in their gifts, and when the time came to move on, we supported them wholeheartedly. Though God has shifted assignments and locations, we are still in touch.

Saying YES to ministry can get messy if you aren't an openhanded leader. Tight-fisted leadership strives to maintain the best ministry while holding on to everyone—clipping their wings per se—allowing them to grow somewhat to serve our vision but never giving them permission to fly and have their own vision. As the body of Christ, we should always see our brothers and sisters in Christ as family, and just as a sibling moving to another place doesn't make them any less family, neither should a member of a ministry or a church moving to a different local church, ministry, or even denomination mean they aren't in the family anymore. If we have a tendency to discommunicate and disassociate with those who leave our organization, we may not have a healthy spiritual family mindset. Healthy families love, support, and stay connected to family members, even if they move—and church families should be the gold standard in this.

Our YES Opens Gifts

So you may have hidden gifts you never knew about. If God is in a purpose, He will make a way. By saying YES to trying ministry, He was our faithful guide in unfamiliar territory. When the season came to shift what our ministry looked like, we began to pray for wisdom on the next steps. Right before the 2020 pandemic halted all events, I had a stirring in me to commission our worship team to write original songs.

> IF GOD IS IN A PURPOSE, HE WILL MAKE A WAY.

After contacting the team, they felt it was within their capacity, and agreed to brainstorm and write whatever came to them. After a few months, no lyrics, melodies, or songs came. I thought maybe I was off on my feeling, and was about to let it go, until everything changed.

Nothing was out of the ordinary about this evening. As I grabbed my toothbrush and commenced my normal bedtime routine, the Lord interrupted me, as He does. Ever notice how He'll show up in an *unusual* way during a very *usual* task?

"Amber, your dad is a songwriter."

Yes.

"Your uncles, aunts, and cousins are songwriters."

Yes.

"You are a songwriter."

What?

"Yes, I've given you this gift."

No.

"Yes."

Jumping into bed, I pondered the unbelievable conversation. *Did I make that up? Do I just so badly want our ministry to release worship songs, I imagined the whole thing?* I quickly found out, I had not. When my head hit the pillow that chilly February night, words flooded my mind, like a dam that had suddenly burst. The lyrics flowed out of me. I laid there about a whole three minutes before I shot up, grabbed my phone, and began typing as fast as my fingers could. With an inquisitive eye, Andrew confusedly asked, "Um, what are you doing?"

"I think I am writing a song." Words I never thought I'd say. Within twenty-four hours the song was complete, on my dad's birthday—the songwriter in my life. God is so timely. The lyrics to "The Secret Place" were written and saved in the notes app on my phone. Weeks later, our country went into a state of emergency and the lyrics remained awaiting, as I lived this song out during the most trying days of our lifetime. During the early months of confusion and worldwide panic, I dwelled in the secret place daily, allowing the presence of God to melt away any fear and chaos, replacing it with peace and boldness. Time at the feet of Jesus does this to a person.

Soon after I penned the lyrics to "The Secret Place," song after song after song came. You should see my running list! I always have one I'm working on. But you want to know something interesting? I am the least musical of my family, and I am not just talking about my immediate family. If you read my first book, *The Awesome One*, you know of my "lack of skills," and how just about my entire extended family is gifted musically, either they have the voice of an angel or can play an instrument incredibly well… and often, it's both. I never learned to play an instrument, but it's on my bucket list, and I was never branded "the best" singer. I was actually told I wasn't.

Maybe you can relate. Is your family or group of friends really good at something, but you feel you can't even bring anything valuable to the table? Musically, I've felt this my whole life. This is why when God unveiled this gift, I cried over and over with gratitude. *Me? Like, me? You gave me this gift? I'm so grateful.* But here is the important thing to take note of: for thirty-six years, I had no idea… and it took a series of saying YES to open it. It makes me wonder, what gifts may be waiting on your table? What will your YES lead to? The journey of saying YES to God will take you to places you never thought you'd go and reveal gifts you never realized you had!

Of course, this songwriting gift wasn't just for me—our gifts and yeses never are. Once I had the songs, we still needed someone to put melodies on them. Shortly after the lyrics arrived, our original worship team dismantled and some now tour nationally. While I'm so proud of them, I wondered if these songs would ever be released. I trusted God anyway, kept writing, and not long after got connected to a worship leader who agreed to take a look. After months of silence on the matter, one day, while strolling through a field, I thought of King David. I prayed, "God, if I am supposed to be like David, singing songs to you out in the field and no one ever hears them, then I will be okay with it. Maybe *You* just want to hear me sing."

> THE JOURNEY OF SAYING YES TO GOD WILL TAKE YOU TO PLACES YOU NEVER THOUGHT YOU'D GO AND REVEAL GIFTS YOU NEVER REALIZED YOU HAD!

After I whispered those heartfelt words, that very day I got a text message containing the first demo of one of my songs. Don't tell me the Lord isn't real. Don't tell me He doesn't hear the cry of our hearts. Look at that timing! He was working behind the scenes and maybe He was just testing my heart. Would I use the gift, even if it was only for Him? Our ministry started hosting worship nights shortly after this and we debuted the song there. I cannot describe what it felt like to have people worshiping my God with the lyrics I wrote just for Him. Undone. I was undone.

As we started putting demos together, we decided to get serious about getting the songs out. We hit our knees: *God, if you want us to release these songs we need you to make a way.* Within a week, we had interviews with not one, but two music producers. What in the actual world?! Soon, I was sitting in meetings with professionals who'd worked with worship teams, produced albums, and even won a Grammy! You talk about feeling out of your element and completely untrained for the task. I had to trust God with the "little" I could bring the table, and He showed up big time.

After selecting our production house and producer, we stepped out, opened United House Worship, recorded our first single, "The Secret Place," by Caleb Fobes and I, and released it in late 2021. Only God. I never thought in a thousand years I would help write a song. I never thought I would have this gift. When I said YES all of those years ago to pray for a friend, I never could have imagined it would have led me here. And the truth is, you never know because God does immeasurably more than we can think, ask, or imagine.

While this gift unfolded, I took a songwriting class where we were told to begin praying to find our "songwriting tribe." I started praying that day. It took a year, but I am so grateful God brought together a fiery group of American and Aussie women to work on the songs, lyrics, and melodies He gives us.

I've since started a record label and, in transparency, I am waiting on the Lord to line other things up to move forward with that company. I hope to partner with more singer/songwriters and musicians, people gifted in all kinds of musical ways, to release worship music and be a resource for those who wish to write and produce songs but don't know the way. I know I can't do all the things, all the time, but I am grateful for the small part I get to play in writing and releasing worship songs for God.

This YES taught our family so much about ministry and what God is capable of with anybody willing to take Him at His word. He doesn't need the most trained or talented, He will bring others who are strong where we aren't. We just say YES and pray for the right people to come alongside and help us with our vision. If it is from God, He will provide. He will make a way. And you might just do something you never dreamed possible, using a gift you never knew you had, to bring glory to the King of kings.

I've got some more tips for your YES journey, you knew I would. These opportunities taught us to, one, pray for God to bring every resource you need to walk out the mission. This can be knowledge, strategies, or people. Most, if not all of your adventures will involve others. Two, God can do a lot with your little. We came with our imperfections and limited experience and the Holy Spirit made up the rest! He needs people to work through, just give Him that. Three, there is a good chance you have a gift you don't even know about. Saying YES to God will reveal more and more of the plans and purposes He has for you. Keep going, it is so exciting to discover the hidden gifts He's placed in you!

> GOD CAN DO A LOT WITH YOUR LITTLE.

Pray for your needs. Show up, and let Him move. Say yes, and discover more gifts.

STRETCHING YOUR YES

SCRIPTURE TO APPLY:
Each of you should use whatever gift you have received to serve others, as faithful stewards of God's grace in its various forms. 1 Peter 4:10 NIV

SONG TO LISTEN:
"The Secret Place," United House Worship

QUESTIONS:
When has God asked you to do something you knew next to nothing about?

Did you let it stop you, or did you follow His lead?

Do you have a gift you haven't used in a while? Share why.

CHALLENGE:
Ask the Holy Spirit if there are any gifts left unopened on your table. They could be stuffed down from the past or you have yet to open them. Write down what you hear/sense. Then, tell a trusted friend and brainstorm on what to do about your gift.

I'LL SAY YES
Even if...
I do not have the money

Are you sure now is the right time for this? I always knew "one day" I'd pursue my dream of owning a coffee shop, but when the doors started opening unexpectedly, I wondered if "one day" had arrived ahead of schedule. The year was 2020, and if you know your history, it wasn't exactly the best time to launch a small business. Restrictions were high and people were staying home more than ever. I had to pray big time.

On one fateful day, I stopped to check out a local donut shop, about forty minutes from my house, and peeking my head inside asked, "How are y'all holding up during the pandemic?" Their response shocked me, "Business is booming."

What?! I couldn't believe it. I was familiar with the local small business, Down for Donuts, because they had the same coffee roaster as us—yes, ya girl had her own custom coffee blends at this point! I have very high coffee bean standards, and God, in His goodness, arranged a divine appointment with Toby and Cheri, owners of Haerfest Coffee Roasting Co. Soon after, they invited us to create our own blends!! I mean, who gets to do that? We didn't just have our own roaster, we had the best, in my opinion, because their beans are not only sourced from high-quality coffee farms from all over the world but are roasted by individuals who have disabilities. The team at Haerfest Roasting company values people with all kinds of abilities and knows how to roast to perfection. I love that our beans have a mission behind them.

Before leaving the Down For Donuts parking lot, I was on the phone with my roaster. "Okay Toby," I asked. "What's it going to take for us to open up our own coffee shop?" He put some numbers together for me, and I put those numbers before God. My mom chimed in and said, "You know where you should put it? In the old florist shop on Old Charlotte Road."

"Take me there!" I enthusiastically declared.

We headed over to take a gander at the recently renovated shop and discovered it had been beautifully updated. I jotted the phone number down from the "For Lease" sign displayed in the window to get more info. Mind you, this was ALL before mentioning anything to Andrew. I spoke with the realtor and after discovering my plans for the building, he eagerly let me know someone could meet me there that evening. I figured it was time to include Andrew in my unfolding plans.

"You know we talked about opening up a coffee shop in like five to ten years? What if we did it now?"

"Huh?"

Then, I laid it all out. The inspiration from the donut joint, rough costs from our roaster, and I even had the location... possibly, and he said, "Well let's go see!"

We toured the potential location that night. As we stood there asking God what we should do, Andrew heard Him speak. Looking in the front window, he could see a cross. In the *natural*, it was a reflection from the church across the street, but in the *supernatural*, it was a sign, accompanied with a Holy Spirit whisper: "I'm in this." Within a few days, we were asked if we wanted the space and they needed an immediate answer, plus the down payment. Apparently, this building was highly sought after; about forty different people and businesses were after it, but the owner wanted "the right" people and business for the space and the neighborhood. Actually, he'd been praying—the entire time he was remodeling—someone would open, wait for it, a coffee shop in his building. Only God y'all.

Every door was opening, but there was only one little problem… We had no money put aside for the down payment OR the cost it would take to open the shop. We heard clearly from God, but we didn't have the actual means to make it happen. We wanted to say YES but also wanted the money there in front of us to make our decision easier. The Holy Spirit kept pushing us to say YES and trust Him to provide; to step out before the way was made—sound familiar?!

So we had this BIG mountain in our way, but we also had a LITTLE bit of faith… and you know what the Word says about that?

Jesus told them. "I tell you the truth, if you had faith even as small as a mustard seed, you could say to this mountain, 'Move from here to there,' and it would move. Nothing would be impossible." Matthew 17:20

We figured, *well since nothing is impossible, let's step out with our mustard seed faith*. We agreed to take the space before we had the actual cash. The day arrived to sign the papers, and within the time we said YES and the meeting was arranged, the money miraculously came in to cover the entire first and last month's rent. Don't forget we were in the middle of a pandemic, and on paper, it was not the best time to start a business, but God knew better. Because of the state of affairs, the government did something unprecedented, sending out thousands of dollars to families all over the country. The stimulus money was deposited in our bank just in time to cover our needs. We still didn't have *all* we needed to open the coffee shop but figured if He provided this far, He'd bring the rest… Our job was trust and agreement. His was the provision.

> **THE ONLY PLAN WE HAD WAS TO SAY YES TO GOD AND WAIT FOR HIM TO BRING WHAT WE NEEDED WHEREVER HE LED US.**

Now, some advised us *not* to go through with the deal unless we had all the funds at the time or at least had a plan to attain it. The only plan we had was to say YES to God and wait for Him to bring what we needed wherever He led us. We decided since our Father owns the cattle on a thousand hills, He could and would provide! We signed without all the funds in hand, but with hearts full of hope and a prayer, *God, Do it again*.

The next morning, we were given the remaining financing we needed. Y'all, when we signed, we had no idea where or when the money would come, but God had us sign before we had the funds—trusting Him to bring it!

If we wait until we have everything we need to pursue a dream, we may never do it. Sometimes if God says go, you just have to go for it, trusting Him to open the doors and bring the provision. Guys, we did this broke but not without hope.

Next, we had to outfit the coffee shop with all the appliances and machines needed for a fraction of the cost. So we did what we always do: when there's a need, we hit our knees. *Alright, Lord, you know our budget and this almost seems impossible, but this is what we got, and we need you to stretch our dollar.* Within days, Andrew found an entire coffee shop set up including machines, a desk, counters, and even beverage and cup supplies. Above and beyond our needs and way BELOW the price we needed it to be. Won't God do it?!

We drove to pick up the equipment and discovered the owners were Christians! Sometimes when negotiating a purchase, we offer lower than asking price, but after prayer, God put it on Andrew's heart to offer the full asking amount and bless them. When we told them what the Lord led us to offer, they cried. This couple was selling it and needed a particular amount to move out west and attend a church ministry *that we regularly learned from*—whose messages had encouraged us over and over in our faith journey. Only God can line things up like this. We're still in touch to this day, and when we go to visit this church, we'll know someone! That day our YES helped make a way for their YES to God!

Over the next few months, God provided every single thing we needed to open our shop. If it was helpers, He put it on peoples' hearts to volunteer their help for a work day. If it was furniture, it was either given, or finances came in unexpectedly to cover it.

I'LL SAY YES

I really wanted to paint wings on the front of the shop, and one day Andrew's cousin Sarah called and said: I'd love to give you money to paint a mural at your coffee shop. I mean EXACTLY what I wanted was done and finances were donated for it.

My favorite provision story has to be the ceiling though. The side dining room ceiling was old, drop tile, office-style, (aka not cute) ceiling, and my design-loving self could not handle this. If it wasn't already obvious our budget wasn't large, so a ceiling wasn't a top priority, but in my heart it was. Andrew basically said unless we get wood for free, we would be keeping the drop-tile ceiling. *Gasp*! I bet you can guess what I did! Oh, I hit those knees again. *Father, I really want a unique ceiling, and I know you can get us some free wood. Make a way!*

Shortly after my prayer, we got the idea to use pallets; they're free! So we started looking… and don't you know, when I wasn't looking for pallets, I had seen them everywhere, but once we were keeping our eyes peeled, ALL the normal spots came up empty! I guess all those bored people during the lockdowns started snatching them up for home projects—because they were gone. So we prayed again, asking where to look. Then, my dad shared a place he'd seen them before. We drove over right away, hoping all the DIYers had not discovered them! I was shocked when we arrived. I had never seen so many pallets on the side of the road in my life, and we quickly got to work loading them up in Andrew's truck. The bed of his F150 overflowed with pallets, piled high to the sky like one of those ridiculous videos you laugh at online.

We got our free wood!! We started cutting the boards and transforming the ceiling, and as we finished, we had so much left over we were able to cover the entire coffee bar and build four planters for our patio… for FREE. God IS able to provide a creative solution when finances are tight!!! He might even give you more than you need!!!

God provided for every single need, and we launched as soon as the restrictions were lifted in July 2020, and it was a hit! It was just what our community needed. Movie theaters and parks had not opened yet, and there weren't many places to gather. Our little neighborhood shop offered the perfect solution! In a time when many places closed their doors, God opened ours—His Kingdom operates by a different set of rules. Just as Allegiance Coffee was a gift to our community, we were given a gift to celebrate our opening. Cheri and Toby, our coffee roasters and friends, presented us with something I'll treasure forever, a custom-made sign which reads: "because she said yes." Story of my life.

Our YES has Impact

So a little yes can have a big impact. We didn't have extra funds for advertising and marketing, but we trusted God to help us, and boy did He! Not long after we opened, we turned some heads. What kind of company opens when others are shutting down? A Kingdom company operating in God's counter-cultural ways, not dictated by the world's system. The day after we launched, we were featured in the biggest newspaper in our state!

Requests started rolling in from local news stations to feature Allegiance Coffee and our story. This was both exciting and a tad nerve-wracking, as we'd never been interviewed by the news before. But the call of God often requires us to step out of our comfort zones, so we said YES. We did interview after interview, some in person, pre-recorded, Zoom, and even LIVE! LIVE television y'all! I never in my life could have imagined this would have grown from a small dream to impact our community to encouraging other small businesses to take a chance during a risky time.

Think of the tiny mustard seed again.

Here is another illustration Jesus used: "<u>The Kingdom of Heaven is like a mustard seed planted</u> in a field. It is the <u>smallest of all seeds, but it becomes the largest of garden plants;</u> it grows into a tree, and birds come and make nests in its branches." Matthew 13:31-32, emphasis added

> **WHEN YOU TAKE YOUR LITTLE AND SOW IT INTO GOD'S KINGDOM, IT CAN GROW BIGGER THAN YOU EVER IMAGINED.**

We didn't have much but our mustard seed faith when we stepped out, but we planted our seed in the garden of God. When you take your little and sow it into God's Kingdom, it can grow bigger than you ever imagined. So while we had no budget for advertising, God started sending news outlets to advertise for us for FREE! They came to us—we didn't even have to lift a finger.

Then, a local magazine released a special piece called the "Best of Charlotte." The article featured local bakeries, restaurants, and coffee shops. When I saw the article, I thought: *I wonder what it would take to get featured in this one day?* I knew it was a pipe dream, but I tend to let my mind dream big. About twenty minutes later, Andrew called me with the most shocking news, "Babe, you aren't going to believe this. One of our customers just came in and said, 'Congratulations on winning the Best of Charlotte!'"

"Huh?!" I was stunned and confused. Quickly jumping on the website I discovered we had won the Editors Choice Award as the Best of Charlotte's coffee shop! (Here's the funny thing, our shop isn't even located in Charlotte!! Haha!) Before I even wished to earn this honor, God had already gone before and blessed like only He can do. Your "little" in God's hands can go way beyond what you ever thought possible.

Because we said YES, Allegiance Coffee has become a blessing to our community. God has used it to create jobs for individuals with disabilities, as a place for other local small businesses to sell their goods, and to give people jobs in a time when it was hard to find one. We saw the impact a coffee shop could have on a city, and we decided to create more opportunities for others to do the same. We now franchise out all our shops and walk new coffee shop owners through the process of running a successful business.

We sold our original location to Anna Cleeland, and she has taken our initial dream and added so much more. She was able to leave her full-time job in the public school system helping oversee individuals with disabilities, to run her own business employing the disabled. She always dreamed of owning her own shop "one day," and it came quicker than she thought (imagine that!). Now Anna gets to offer an equal opportunity job to adults with a disability. Our YES led to hers.

This YES taught me God's timing may not be yours and the value of seizing the moment. The anointing to open the coffee shop was for 2020. I had to say YES then, otherwise, the story wouldn't have been quite as miraculous. When doors begin to open, we need to pay attention, even if it doesn't make sense to us. I learned to see Proverbs 3:5-6 in a whole new light.

Trust in the LORD with all your heart; do not depend on your own understanding. Seek his will in all you do, and he will show you which path to take.

> WHEN DOORS BEGIN TO OPEN, WE NEED TO PAY ATTENTION, EVEN IF IT DOESN'T MAKE SENSE TO US.

I have to smile while wrapping up this chapter. While writing my last book, I would frequently escape to my favorite local coffee shop located in the small town God asked us to give up to follow Him to North Carolina. Now completing this book, I'm typing away in *our* coffee shop. Full circle.

This opportunity left me with ALL the tips, y'all. First, don't depend on what you know, depend on God! He can do all things. He has all resources available to Him, and when we're in a partnership, this means we have access to those resources. Second, don't let what you see in the natural ever stop you from pursuing a God-dream; if the timing is right, He will make a way! When we say YES and have just a little bit of faith, we position ourselves to see mountain-moving miracles.

Third, you do not have to possess all the money to make the dream happen, but you do have to hear clearly from the Holy Spirit about the matter. We weren't walking in blind, God spoke to us. Our faith sprung from His word to us. Fourth, if finances are an issue, pray to the Lord and ask for creative solutions. This gives God an opportunity to show off and blow your mind with His creativity and provision. Fifth, do not be intimidated by the enormity of the opportunity. When we heard the first estimate of costs or got asked to be on LIVE television where there would be no edit if we messed up, we could have declined. We could have seen the mountain and bowed out... but we didn't and neither can you! If you believe God can do anything, then kick fear to the curb and ask God to turn you into a mountain conqueror. Draw on the strength of Jesus who is in you. Let Him empower you to take the ground!

Depend on God. See with eyes of faith. You don't need the money, you need the Lord. Pray for unique solutions. Don't be intimidated!

STRETCHING YOUR YES

SCRIPTURE TO APPLY:
And God will generously provide all you need. Then you will always have everything you need and plenty left over to share with others.
2 Corinthians 9:8

SONG TO LISTEN:
"Jireh," Elevation Worship & Maverick City

QUESTIONS:
How do you respond when God's timeline and yours do not match?

Do you find yourself more inclined to walk by faith or by sight?

Name one lesson you learned from this story to help you trust the Lord to provide where He guides.

Share about a time when God did something for you that you were unable to do for yourself.

CHALLENGE:
The next time God puts a dream in your heart, pray and ask Him if it's for now or the future. If it's huge and expensive, don't immediately write it off. If you sense it is a "pursue right now" dream, say YES and start giving God something to work with. Meaning: The Lord is able to shut something down if the timing isn't correct, but one way to test the waters is to dip our toes in. If He clears the way and begins to align things, it might be time.

12

I'LL SAY YES
Even if...
I don't like it

It's really hard to write in this environment. I pushed back when God said it was time to start writing *I'll Say Yes*. I wanted to wait until the circumstances were more conducive to my creativity to begin this assignment. When I wrote my last book, *The Awesome One*, I had a private office with a glorious fireplace and perfectly positioned bookshelves filled with all my favorite works. It overlooked a grove of beautiful trees—always showcasing the beauty of each season, blooming in the spring, full of lush green leaves in the summer, painted with color in the fall, and snow-laden branches in the winter—I have a thing for trees. There is something majestic about them that causes me to ponder: *Wow, how amazing is our God that He spoke those into existence. I mean, WHAT!?* Just think, one little acorn has all the potential to grow into the massive towering oak it will become. Incredible. And God made this with His mouth. His. Mouth. I mean what kind of powerful God do we serve?!

The last time I undertook the book-writing task it was uncomplicated. I was surrounded by beauty and inspiration. It's easy to write in a picturesque setting. This time, I'm writing in a camper... and just so I paint the picture crystal clear for you: I don't even like camping. Haha. Truth be told, I put off writing this book because I wanted to be in my long-awaited "forever house," writing in the office I've been dreaming of and designing—on my Pinterest board, of course. How simple would it be to write in an immaculately designed writing space, steaming hot cup of coffee in hand, filled with cute decor, and the wall covered with perfect writing quotes in white frames, inspiring every stroke of my pen? If only. But that is not where I am writing. I find myself sitting on a bed because there is nowhere else to write once everyone is asleep, the lights are off and all the beds are pulled out because we all sleep in the camper. And I don't like to camp. Did I say that already? Just making sure you feel me.

But I can't wait to write when things are perfect because the passion to write this book is burning in me now. And while the circumstances are less than ideal, perhaps God needed me to write and release this book in this season for a reason.

> I HAVE HAD TO LEARN TO NOT LET MY SURROUNDINGS DICTATE MY CREATIVITY.

The truth is, sometimes saying YES to God takes us places we don't expect. However, this unexpected leg of my journey has done more in me than I ever knew I needed. For starters, I've learned that if I can write in this environment, I can write in any place! If I successfully complete a whole book in an uninspiring location, then this tells me I'll be able to do it anywhere, in any circumstance. I have had to learn to not let my surroundings dictate my creativity, and I think this is a gift I wouldn't have found in a place of beauty.

Think about Paul y'all, he wrote some of the most inspirational words, which still impact us today from prison. I mean if he can write…

… I have learned to be content whatever the circumstances. I know what it is to be in need, and I know what it is to have plenty. I have learned the secret of being content in any and every situation, whether well fed or hungry, whether living in plenty or in want. I can do all this through him who gives me strength… Philippians 4:11-13 NIV

… from jail, obviously, he found something greater than his surroundings to inspire—and so must we.

There is a temptation to let the seasons of life dictate our creativity. Easy times encourage our calling while hard times discourage our purpose—often causing us to shelf a project, a dream, a YES. But I say no more.

So how did we get here, a non-camping family living in a camper? We listened to God and felt Him guiding us to move out of our previous neighborhood; We said, YES, we'll move. We were only supposed to live here for a month until we found our house. Then, the housing market skyrocketed during the 2020-21 pandemic and it became impossible to find what we were looking for at the price we wanted. It was definitely a seller's market. So we got stuck in limbo.

So while sometimes saying YES to God is exciting and glamorous, sometimes it looks like living in an RV. Sometimes, it feels like being a nomad. Sometimes, it looks like camping in a wilderness with no end in sight. The Israelites know about the "wilderness" season and so does anyone who has ever done anything for God. But you know what I find so interesting about wilderness seasons?

God leads His people there. Check out these two examples from the Bible:

The Israelites left Succoth and camped at Etham on the edge of the wilderness. The LORD went ahead of them. He guided them during the day with a pillar of cloud, and he provided light at night with a pillar of fire. This allowed them to travel by day or night. Exodus 13:20-21

Then Jesus, full of the Holy Spirit, returned from the Jordan River. He was led by the Spirit in the wilderness… Luke 4:1

Often, when we find ourselves in the "wilderness" season, it feels like maybe we made a wrong turn, but I see time and time again in the Word that God takes His people there to work out "some things." Saying YES will take us to fun and exciting places but it will also take us to necessary spots—places where we learn lessons which can only be taught in the wild.

> **NO MATTER WHAT SEASON WE FIND OURSELVES IN, WE MUST LET THE SEASON DO ITS WORK.**

No matter what season we find ourselves in, we must let the season do its work. God takes us through different seasons in our life. The hidden season, the wilderness season, the dry season, the waiting season, the fiery trial season, the fruitful season, the frontlines season, the training season, and there are others. Some of these seasons are often combined. Most of the time, we are led by God on this journey, and occasionally, we fall into these seasons because of a misstep or attack.

As a believer, no matter how we got to a particular season, we can take comfort in knowing He will never leave us or forsake us, and He causes all things to work together for the good of those who love Him (Deuteronomy 31:6, Romans 8:28). But regardless of how we "got here," in every season, we *must* let the season work something out of us.

Naturally, when the fiery wilderness trials come, we want to run away, but what if there is a greater purpose in this fire? What if the flame isn't meant to burn us, but to purify us? Psalm 66:10 says, "You have tested us, O God; you have purified us like silver." When we pair this truth with the following parable, we discover that refining is making us stronger, and the work God is doing isn't merely for our own benefit.

"The Kingdom of Heaven is like a mustard seed planted in a field. It is the smallest of all seeds, <u>but it becomes the largest of garden plants; it grows into a tree, and birds come and make nests in its branches.</u>"

We need to realize our trials aren't just for us. As God uses them to work something out of us, He does something in us… We are growing. Our roots are going down deep and our branches are stretching up high. When we allow the trials to develop us, we become a safe place for others to flock to. Did you notice how birds come to the tree to rest? And so, people will flock to us and find safety and comfort in our presence… why? Because we've allowed God to purify us and fill us with His character and presence during the wilderness, when we come out of the trial—and we will come out—we can offer comfort, help, and deliverance to others going through their trials!

I'll Say Yes

Grace for our YES

So God can supply you with grace for your season. I'm sure you'd love to know what God worked out of me during the RV living/Wilderness season. MANY things, let me tell you. I already mentioned how I learned to write in any atmosphere, but God did some deeper work in me. I realized I was banking my happiness on my home. While having a house is essential, it should never be what brings us contentment. If we let our home be our source of joy or peace, what happens when we no longer have it? Well, I found out. Haha! I was discouraged and discontent for a little while… Let me tell you how God opened my eyes to my displaced contentment.

God, why don't you just open a door for me to have a home?! I am mad at you! I know you can move mountains, why don't you just make a way for us to get a house? I'm frustrated, I'm hurt, and so discouraged. I prayed in despair, then stormed out of the camper slamming the door for dramatic effect.

Next, I did the most godly thing… I opened my phone and started scrolling because this *always* helps when you're feeling discontent with your life. Insert rolling eyes emoji. Do you know what the first thing that popped on my feed was? A sermon clip from a Pastor who has blessed my life over and over, and do you know what He said?

"Sometimes we want things so bad we are not going to be happy unless it happens our way. 'I can't be happy unless I get the house, unless I meet the right person, unless we have the baby.' That's out of balance. Anything you have to have in order to be happy the Enemy can use against you. And it's good to be honest with God, tell Him your dreams, tell Him what you are believing for…

It's fine to ask, but then be mature enough to say, 'But God, if it never happens… I'm still going to trust you.' See, we can get so consumed by what we want, it can become like an idol. It's all we think about, it's all we pray about, it's always on the forefront of our minds. Turn it over to God. Pray. Believe. Then leave it in God's hands. Don't get so focused on what you want that you miss the beauty of this day. Everything may not be perfect. There are things that need to change. But God has given you the grace to be happy today." - Pastor Joel Osteen[4]

Ummmmmmmm if that wasn't a timely word from the Lord, I don't know what is. Not only was I unhappy because of where I lived but how about the first thing he mentions is "if you aren't happy unless you get the house!" Well, just call me out Holy Spirit! Not only that, Pastor Joel even shared about how obsessing over what we want could be a sign that we've made it an idol! Wow. Cut me up and down! But, that is exactly what I had done, and I had no idea. I was completely basing my contentment on my home situation, which is dangerous. Living this way means when I have a beautiful home, I am happy and when I am living in a less-than-ideal home, I would be sad and discouraged. What had I become? A person who lets surroundings determine happiness: Unstable.

I apologized right there on the spot. I told God I was sorry for deriving my contentment from anything other than Him. I then asked Him to give me the grace for my current living situation, and y'all won't believe what happened!! He instantly supplied it. I was full of joy again. I was happy as a lark, and I could even laugh about where I lived knowing it was in God's hands and He knew what He was doing. God was the object of my affection again, the foundation for my happiness, the source of joy.

In the wilderness, I truly found joy in the Lord alone (because I had to), but now that He was the only source, it could never be taken from me. What a hard but necessary lesson and only one I could learn in a camper in the wilderness. Sometimes, we need to give up what we think is best for us to truly live our "best life." Maybe this is what Jesus meant when He said:

If you try to hang on to your life, you will lose it. But if you give up your life for my sake, you will save it. Matthew 16:25

When we follow His lead into the wilderness and embrace the purification process, we might just develop the character and have the heart change needed to withstand anything life throws at us—learning to live life to the fullest in every situation. What a gift.

The funny thing is, I didn't even know I needed to deal with this problem. We often don't until we're delivered. We need to flip the script on these wilderness seasons. Let's start letting them work something out of us, reveal the impurities which have taken root in our hearts, and replace the discouragement with grace to endure the process.

Let whatever season you find yourself in do the work. Don't avoid the fire of purification, let it burn those impurities out. Instead of leading you to despair, let the demand of the season point you to your supply of grace for ANY circumstance.

This YES taught me the importance of listening to God even if I don't like where He takes me. Contrary to what culture tells you, life won't always look how you picture it. When we submit to God being our guide, it will be both amazing and challenging.

Even if... *I don't like it*

I would be remiss if I said living a life of saying YES is always a walk in the park. This isn't Biblical or true. In John 16:33b (NIV) Jesus said, "In this world you will have trouble. But take heart! I have overcome the world." Since He is in us, we can overcome, too. In the hard seasons, we learn to rely on the strength of Christ. As we discover the secret to contentment is not found in our situation or surroundings, but in our God, we become unshakable. What a gift. This refining season taught me to say YES to the exciting AND the hard.

> DON'T AVOID THE FIRE OF PURIFICATION, LET IT BURN THOSE IMPURITIES OUT.

Doing it all with God, trusting Him as your good and faithful guide. It's all worth it.

STRETCHING YOUR YES

SCRIPTURE TO APPLY:
But he knows where I am going. And when he tests me, I will come out as pure as gold. Job 23:10

SONG TO LISTEN:
"Refiner," Maverick City Music

QUESTIONS:
Have you ever been or do you find yourself currently in a refining or wilderness season? Explain.

What has God been working out in you in this time? (Or what *did* He work out?)

How has this chapter challenged you to embrace a difficult season?

Have you ever said YES to a difficult request from the Lord? Share about it.

CHALLENGE:
When you find yourself in a difficult season, instead of asking, "Why?" say, "What are you trying to teach me here?" and "What are you doing in me?" Then, be sure to pray for the grace to endure!

I'LL SAY YES

Even if...
I am not a pastor

"Ummmmmm I'd love to, but you know I'm not an ordained pastor, right?" I was both eager to be the camp pastor and unsure if I could be. When the director of the Wings of Eagles summer camp asked Andrew and me to lead chapel for the week, I had to let her know we didn't have qualifications, on paper, for such a task—even so, my heart was on fire with His Word. I braced for Christine's response and instead of rejection, it was acceptance.

"But, you love Jesus, and that's all that matters." Her words affirmed us more than she knew. We said YES and prayed for the Lord to use us. And boy did He show up. Each day, He gave us the exact scripture and message, and each day, the kids, volunteers, and adults responded. I was a little surprised, not that God was moving, but that He was using us, of all people.

Every morning, we planned our lesson, but we were always willing to shift if the Holy Spirit led in a different way—He did. One morning, we had a plan, but as soon as we arrived, God made adjustments. Andrew headed down to the outdoor chapel and began reading the prayer popsicle sticks strung across the front of the space, tethered to a wooden cross. There was a recurring request: anxiety, anxiousness, fear, anxiety disorder. At the same time, I was talking with Christine, the director, in another location and she wanted us to be aware of the weight of anxiety and fear in the camp. I took note and headed down to the chapel as worship was starting. I leaned over to Andrew and whispered, "I know we had planned to speak on something else, but I feel God is saying we have to address anxiety." Surprise and confirmation washed over him as he responded, "God told me the same thing."

Let's go!!!

Years prior to this moment, Andrew and I had battled intense anxiety in our family, both in my husband and with our son having night terrors, and we shared our stories at camp that morning. We told them how we got the victory in each situation. We declared with boldness, "As a Christian, anxiety is not your identity. You do not have anxiety, you have Jesus. You are not fearful, you are in Christ. It is time to break ties with this lie. Fear might come on you, but it is not *yours*. God did not give you a spirit of fear, but of power, love, and sound mind, and we're going to teach you how to fight fear!" Every eye was locked on us, and you could have heard a pin drop. We had the room and unleashed the Heavenly strategy God had given us in that season—a tangible tool to beat the spirit of fear. When we gave the altar call for anyone who wanted to pray to be set free from anxiety, it was FULL of people, from five-year-olds to adults.

What happened? That morning we had a plan, but God had another, and since we've decided to be available to what He is doing, to allow our agenda to be interrupted with His, we let the Spirit lead. When you partner with what God is doing in the moment, you make room for the miraculous.

Jesus modeled this regularly. Once, He was on the way to heal a local synagogue leader's daughter when He suddenly came to a halt as He felt power go out from Him. Now, Jairus' little girl was on her deathbed, and he did not have a moment to waste—but the Heavenly Father had a bigger plan in the moment, and Jesus partnered with Him to see even greater deliverance.

> WHEN YOU PARTNER WITH WHAT GOD IS DOING IN THE MOMENT, YOU MAKE ROOM FOR THE MIRACULOUS.

Let's pick up the story in Luke 8.

"Who touched me?" Jesus asked.

Everyone denied it, and Peter said, "Master, this whole crowd is pressing up against you."

But Jesus said, "Someone deliberately touched me, for I felt healing power go out from me." When the woman realized that she could not stay hidden, she began to tremble and fell to her knees in front of him. The whole crowd heard her explain why she had touched him and that she had been immediately healed. "Daughter," he said to her, "your faith has made you well. Go in peace."

While he was still speaking to her, a messenger arrived from the home of Jairus, the leader of the synagogue. He told him, "Your daughter is dead. There's no use troubling the Teacher now."

But when Jesus heard what had happened, he said to Jairus, "Don't be afraid. Just have faith, and she will be healed."

When they arrived at the house, Jesus wouldn't let anyone go in with him except Peter, John, James, and the little girl's father and mother. The house was filled with people weeping and wailing, but he said, "Stop the weeping! She isn't dead; she's only asleep."

But the crowd laughed at him because they all knew she had died. Then Jesus took her by the hand and said in a loud voice, "My child, get up!" And at that moment her life returned, and she immediately stood up! Luke 8:45-55a

As you can see from the passage, Jesus wanted to acknowledge in front of everyone *who* got healed. She tried to hide. We can guess why. Since this woman bled constantly, she was considered "unclean." Anyone who touched her would also be deemed unclean, and she should not have been in that crowd according to their customs. Not only that but if she was unclean, she wouldn't have been permitted to worship in the "local synagogue." Oh, wait, who was Jairus? A leader of the local synagogue. For twelve years, this unclean woman would have been turned away from worshiping in the community. Do you think Jairus knew who she was? I believe so.

Next, we see something very precious. Jesus first calls her daughter, no doubt healing a deeper heart issue, and then makes another important statement: your faith has made you well. The crowd knew who she was. Jairus knew who she was. God knew who she was. When Jesus revealed her faith made her well, He was displaying how faith is connected to healing. He was using the moment to teach Jairus something about mountain-moving faith. To believe God was able to heal what no doctor can. To believe against all odds for the miraculous.

Next, a messenger arrives from Jairus' house with news, *He told him, "Your daughter is dead. There's no use troubling the Teacher now."*

But when Jesus heard what had happened, he said to Jairus, "Don't be afraid. Just have faith, and she will be healed."

God is so strategic! Jesus partnered with the plan of the Father in a moment, not to delay His arrival at Jairus' house but instead to build his faith by performing a miracle right in front of him. See, Jesus could have kept walking, knowing the woman was healed and not acknowledged it, but then He would have missed an opportunity to build Jairus' faith. I believe since he probably knew the woman and knew of her incurable ailment, when he saw God heal this "daughter," it confirmed Jesus could heal his. Jairus' faith skyrocketed and of course, Jesus did heal his precious child. Partnering with what the Holy Spirit is doing in a moment, even if it seems like a delay, paves the way for the power of God to be displayed!

The week we spoke at summer camp, God showed up and led in an unexpected direction, but as we followed, His presence was confirmed. The Spirit poured throughout the entire week and everyone was touched. The kids needed it, the leaders needed it, and we needed it. This generation doesn't need to just "hear about what God did," they need to experience Him moving now. God showed Himself to be real, using two unordained pastors who were just willing to be vessels.

> THIS GENERATION DOESN'T NEED TO JUST "HEAR ABOUT WHAT GOD DID," THEY NEED TO EXPERIENCE HIM MOVING NOW.

Saying YES to being the camp pastors taught us to go where the Spirit leads and say what He says. It also showed me the importance of partnering with God to overcome every battle that comes your way because, once you learn Heaven's blueprint for getting freedom, you can teach it to others.

Engage the battle with YES

So regular people can minister for the Lord. Have you ever felt called to do something for God but talked yourself out of it because you aren't on staff at a church? Camp pastor was not the only time I pulled this excuse card out. Recently, I felt God calling me to share what I was learning online—but I pushed back. I came up with every reason not to share:

- No one listens to me
- I don't have any platform
- If spiritual leaders don't acknowledge my gift, maybe I don't have one
- When I share, I only get one comment

However, my perspective shifted in one service. God spoke to me during worship and through our pastor. The Lord always communicates super clearly with me while I'm singing. I don't know why this is, but this is when I hear His voice crystal clear. "You've sheathed your sword."

This is all He said… but I knew it was the Holy Spirit, and I knew He was right. Wielding the Sword of the Spirit, which is the Word of God, is my absolute favorite thing. When I hear those Christian comedians poke fun at believers who always use the Word in every situation (from finding good parking spots to stumbling upon the best sale—they can somehow fit a Bible verse into every situation), yeah, I am *that* girl! I literally always have the Word in my heart and on my lips. If you have an issue, I got a verse for you.

After facing some intense persecution, I got insecure and stopped sharing scripture publicly. God showed up on the scene that day to wake me up. He didn't stop there. Our pastor then unpacked a familiar passage in a fresh way. The exact way I needed.

Abram believed the LORD, and He credited it to Him as righteousness. Genesis 15:6 NIV

He went on to unpack one word, and it left a mark on my life. Guess which one? "Believed." I bet you didn't think I was going there. I surely would not have picked this to be the life-changing word. But it was. He said in Hebrew it actually means "to foster," and encouraged us to "act as if we already had" what we're believing God for.

As a person who doesn't have a large platform—according to the world's standards—who also dreams of having an impactful ministry, I have questioned whether my words make a difference. I heard this message, circled back to my excuses then considered what God had said. Do I unsheath my sword? Do I act as though I already have impact? And if so, what would I do if I did have an influential ministry? Would I share the Word consistently? YES. Would I encourage people regardless of comments? YES. Would I wait for a Christian leader to give me permission to share about Jesus? NO! But would I start telling anyone who would listen with or without someone's stamp of approval? YES!

I'LL SAY YES

God shook me awake, and I said YES to His call. I decided to share without the numbers, without the ministry, without the stamp of approval, and I chose to act as if I had it all—because I did. The parable of the lost sheep in Matthew 18 gave me confidence.

If a man has a hundred sheep and <u>one of them</u> wanders away, what will he do? Won't he leave the ninety-nine others on the hills and <u>go out to search for the one that is lost</u>? And if he finds it, I tell you the truth, <u>he will rejoice over it more than over the ninety-nine</u> that didn't wander away! In the same way, it is not my heavenly Father's will that <u>even one</u> of these little ones should perish.

God values the one and so should we. The Lord showed me that many are after the crowd, the numbers, the likes, but He asked, "Would you still minister if it's only for one? If only one person is impacted? Not many will."

I was determined to encourage people even if only one person responded because Jesus would. He would give up the crowd to hunt down and bless the one. The Good Shepherd rejoices more over one than a huge group, so it seems in His Kingdom numbers are calculated differently. Starting small, blessing one is not only okay but exactly what we need to do! It's not about the platform, but about the message. It is about people hearing about a God who loves them and a Savior who came for them, and I couldn't let excuses keep me from saying YES.

> **GOD VALUES THE ONE AND SO SHOULD WE.**

The next day as I was pondering the statement God had made the day before, *"You have sheathed your sword..."* then, He continued...

"but you're not the only one. Many of my children have been discouraged and dismayed by this season of waiting, pain, and struggle. They feel dry. They are wandering in the wilderness as they wait on their promise. And they put their swords down.

But they must not.

They must not put down their sword. They must not put it away. They must pull out the divine weapon of God and use it to fight this spiritual battle. Make no mistake, they are in a spiritual war and those are only won with spiritual weapons.

The Sword of the Spirit is the most underutilized weapon in my children.

It is a gift of highest worth. When they wield the Sword of the Spirit—which means to speak the Word out of their mouth—they cut through the Enemy's defenses. WHEN MY WORD IS ON THEIR LIPS AGAIN THE TIDE WILL TURN. Use my Word and see the victory!

Jesus, your King, showed you how to wield the Sword well.

He said: "It is written..." spoke scripture with power, and the Devil had to leave. It will do the same for you. (Matthew 4 and Luke 4)

"They have overcame him by the blood of the Lamb and by the word of their testimony..." Revelation 12:11 NKJV

We are the sons and the daughters of God—Jesus sacrificed His blood to give us authority over the Enemy, now it is up to us to use our weapon: His Word on our lips!

His blood, our Words.

I'll SAY YES

His blood, our Words."

So while the message of pulling out my sword was for me, it was for you too, and all of God's children who have put down our most potent weapon. So I charge you to pick it up. Say YES to using God's Word to fight the battle.

This was the first thing I shared publicly after God recommissioned me and unlocked my mouth, and the response was more than I ever would have thought. People shared it. People asked me questions. People sent me messages about using the Sword of the Spirit. People asked for scriptures to battle. I. Was. Shocked. I said YES even though I doubted my words would make an impact, but they did.

Saying YES when I didn't have a platform or man's stamp of approval taught me God uses anyone who is willing, regardless of followers and man's system. He reminded me the religious elite of Jesus' day didn't approve of Him either, but His heavenly Father sure did. If Jesus didn't need a person's approval, then neither do we. If we're waiting on the numbers to be right or the approval to come, we may never start sharing... but think of all the people we could miss because we waited. Share for the one!

While I honor and am grateful for the healthy spiritual leadership I've experienced in my life, we don't have to wait to be validated by a person to be used by God. We just need to say YES when He prompts us to share His message.

My tips for saying YES when you don't feel as spiritually equipped or supported are first, follow when and where the Spirit leads. Be flexible with your plan and message, always giving God permission to change it as needed. Second, always ask God what He is doing in the room. What does He want to accomplish? Partner with that answer. Third, give others what He is teaching you, and don't worry about the outcome. Obedience is our job, the outcome is His. You don't have to overcomplicate sharing Biblical truths. If you just share your "daily bread" with others, it becomes very easy to be a witness.

Be Spirit-led. Ask God the plan. Share what God is teaching you.

STRETCHING YOUR YES

SCRIPTURE TO APPLY:
Is not this the kind of fasting I have chosen: to loose the chains of injustice and untie the cords of the yoke, to set the oppressed free and break every yoke? Is it not to share your food with the hungry... Isaiah 58:6-7 NIV

SONG TO LISTEN:
"Holy Ground," Passion

QUESTIONS:
Have you ever wanted to share something God is teaching you but felt as though no one would listen? Did you share and/or push past the insecurity?

When the Holy Spirit leads you to step out, are you more inclined to offer excuses of why you can't, or do you embrace the mandate right away?

What do you sense God is calling you to do right now?

Share one step you can take towards the purpose the Lord has for your life.

CHALLENGE:
This week, share your "daily bread" at least one time with others. This could be online through a video, image, short devotional, or in-person. Your thoughts matter. Your revelations matter. Your witness matters.

14

I'LL SAY YES
Even if...
I don't know how it's going to work out

Wait, you want me to do WHAT? I knew what God had said, but since this would be a bold move, I still felt the need for a blinking neon sign, confirming the right direction.

"Make the conference free."

My eyes were as wide as saucers, and I just stood there staring at my Bible. My team and I had been preparing for a women's conference, and truthfully, I didn't know if anyone would come. I felt God calling me to host one, and y'all know I said YES, feeling unqualified and all, but by this time, I was fully trusting He would show up, as He always does. But now He done went too far. *Free?!* We had expenses! Mouths to feed. Supplies to buy. Shirts to purchase. Speakers and a worship team to pay. *Lord, free?!*

But I could not deny the tugging of the Holy Spirit as I read the words of Jesus:

When you put on a luncheon or a banquet," he said, *"don't invite your friends, brothers, relatives, and rich neighbors. For they will invite you back,* *and that will be your only reward. <u>Instead, invite the poor, the crippled, the lame, and the blind.</u> Then at the resurrection of the righteous, God will reward you for inviting those who could not repay you.* Luke 14:12-14, emphasis added

The Light Conference would be a banquet of the Word of God and the Spirit, of Jesus and soul cleansing and healing balm, a feast of spiritual bread, oil, and wine. We had originally set our ticket price to cover all our expenses, but the Lord was leading me to return the money to pre-purchased tickets and make the event free. I immediately jumped on the phone with two people, my husband and then General Manager/friend/cohort of all "my things," Jessica—both of whom are very budget conscious and logical, and they both replied: If God said it has to be free, then make it free. I knew with both of them on board, this was God! Us all in agreement was all the confirmation I needed.

We had to make this women's conference attainable for any woman to come, and we were determined to trust the Lord. He doesn't make people pay to hear good news. He doesn't ask me to give Him money at the door of Heaven when I come and dine with Him, and I needed to make sure anyone could be ministered to, whether poor or rich. We went into the conference with a few hundred dollars, and we needed a few thousand to just cover expenses. We stepped out in faith, said YES to His leading, prayed, and believed.

I felt like the woman in the parable of the yeast.

Jesus also used this illustration: "The Kingdom of Heaven is like the yeast a woman used in making bread. Even though <u>she put only a little yeast in three measures of flour, it permeated every part of the dough.</u>"

Our team wasn't professionally trained to run a conference, and we sure didn't have a lot of money to put one on. Not one of us was an ordained pastor, but we all loved Jesus and knew God could do a lot with our little. Like the woman who took just a pinch of yeast and threw it into a large batch of dough, the tiny amount spread!

He put His big on our little and, as The Light Conference commenced, it is hard to explain what God did before our very eyes. Miracle after miracle after miracle. First, a ton of women showed up, I didn't know if twenty would. They came from all over the country. California, Michigan, Texas, Indiana, Oklahoma, Tennessee, and South Carolina! People who were not supposed to attend, somehow heard about it, through friends and online chat rooms. God lined up divine appointments. He sent words of confirmation and affirmation. He stepped in and lit fires in each person's life.

I wanted it to be so special for the ladies and even had this vision of one long table for all the women to sit at, representing a banquet in the Kingdom, representing how we all had a seat in God's house. I knew what a meal like this would cost, and I also believed God could make it happen. My desire was to provide snacks the entire time for women, y'all know ladies like to nibble and have plenty of coffee. Well, guess what? We had it all AND, get this, it was completely FREE. Yes, you heard that right. Someone donated and cooked and set up all the snacks, a full gourmet, organic brunch, AND an over-the-top, delicious lunch. This was not someone attending the event, just a woman of God who heard about the conference and wanted to donate her time, the food God had given her, and use her gift to bless the body of Christ. Only God. He sure loves on His daughters well.

But this isn't all. My church let us use their facility for a fraction of the cost. All praise to Him. We sold merchandise and took donations from vendors to help as much as we could, but as we neared the end of the event, we still needed several thousand dollars. God knew our need, and we kept going.

Our Yes, His Provision

At the last session, we felt led to open the floor for a good ol' testimony time. From teenagers to grandmas, woman after woman got up to share what God had done over the weekend. Not one of them faltered over their words, sharing stories of the faithfulness of God they had never rehearsed. The comfort in the room was evident. Have you ever gone to an event where a few heard from God but some left not really experiencing Him move? This was not like that. EVERYONE had a story, and I mean everyone. God moved in all of us. As I sat there listening to the stories, I was overwhelmed with the goodness of our Lord. He ministered to every single person.

One lady took the mic and shared an incredible story. She told us how she was supposed to be at a conference in New England, not here. But on the way to the airport, the entire place lost power and EVERY flight was canceled. Who has even heard of that?! She had been looking forward to getting away to connect with God, and when she heard of another women's conference, she jumped in her car and decided to attend ours because it was, get this: FREE. Now, what if I had said NO to God and not made it free? She would have never been there.

Near the end of the event, we told the ladies how God had put it on our hearts to make the event free, but if He had deposited something in them at the event and they wanted to sow into our ministry, we still had some costs to cover. Afterward, the lady who was not supposed to be there came up and asked how much we needed. After some quick calculations with Jessica, we came up with the total needed. It was a lot. We thought of telling her a lesser amount because it seemed too much… but we knew we had to tell her about it all. We told her what we needed and she said, "I'll cover it all." WHAT?! I mean what?! Can you even? God literally shut down an entire airport, redirected this woman so He could meet her at our conference, then He prompted her to pay the rest of our expenses! ONLY. GOD.

This YES taught me God can and will provide as we are faithful to do exactly as He says. When we say YES and believe God for the impossible, we get to see miracles. Sometimes, God leads us to do big things not knowing how they will turn out and if anyone will come, but whether it's one or hundreds, each person matters to Him. One small YES can later turn into big ones.

Do you think I ever pictured myself leading a women's conference? Heck no. When I started my YES journey, I didn't even want to pray with one of my friends out loud, let alone pray over hundreds of strangers. I didn't blindly step out in faith to God prompting me to make the event free because I hoped He would come through; No, I knew He would. Each YES showed me something about Him: He could be trusted. Where he guided, He always provided.

Leading a conference provided more tips for my collection. First, you must know that a small YES will lead to a big YES eventually, but we have to be faithful with the little before He gives us the large. And even then, what God considers big might

> A SMALL YES WILL LEAD TO A BIG YES EVENTUALLY, BUT WE HAVE TO BE FAITHFUL WITH THE LITTLE BEFORE HE GIVES US THE LARGE.

appear to us to as something small… like telling a stranger of His love, but this could stop them from ending their life. Nothing is insignificant in His Kingdom. Don't underestimate the power of your YES and who it might affect. Second, if God says it, do it, even if it doesn't make sense. I recommend getting confirmation if you're not sure, as I did in my story. Third, don't put a limit on the provision of God. He can shut down airports and have grocery stores hear about your situation and meet your needs. All provisions and resources are in His hands.

Say YES to the small. Do what God says. Trust He can provide.

STRETCHING YOUR YES

SCRIPTURE TO APPLY:
And my God shall supply all your need according to his riches in glory by Christ Jesus. Philippians 4:19 KJV

SONG TO LISTEN:
"Million Little Miracles," Elevation Worship & Maverick City Music

QUESTIONS:
Do you hope to do more "small" or "big" opportunities for God? Why?

When the Holy Spirit leads you to do something that makes no sense, how do you typically respond? Blind faith? Question it? Explain.

What helps you to have the courage to step out in faith?

Share about a time God miraculously provided for you.

CHALLENGE:
The next time you are sure the Lord is leading you to do something that doesn't make sense logically... trust His guidance. Get Confirmation and find a promise to stand on.

15

I'LL SAY YES
Even if...
It's not what I expected

Since this is way out in left field, I'll know this is you, God, if you have Andrew lean over and say this exact vision to me. I internally struggled with a picture I'd just envisioned. Deep in worship at church, the Lord interrupted—like He does—and asked me a question I did not expect.

"Would you give up your dream house for me?"

The question shocked me, so I didn't respond instantly.

I felt a great stretching take place within me. We had lived unexpectedly in the old camper for one and half years, and y'all know how I felt about camping. I was ready to get out. The Saturday evening before He posed this audacious question, I had an epiphany. The entire time we'd been in our "camping in the wilderness" season, I had been praying for our farmhouse or any house for that matter. We tried renting, no luck. We tried land contracts, fell through. We tried getting a mortgage, wasn't happening. For months, we had tried everything, and I had been asking for what I wanted. Never once did I ask God what He wanted for us in this time. What was I thinking? As soon as I realized it, I instantly got on my knees and asked Him, *Father, all this time I've been asking you for what I want. I'm sorry. Let me correct my prayer. What do you want for us?*

The next morning, He answered. It was not what I planned or expected. During worship, I heard the familiar heavenly whisper, "Would you travel for me?"

Yes, of course! And then He popped the shocking question:

"Would you give up your dream house for me?"

I *didn't* want to give up this dream—especially since I felt He promised one day I would have this. But, I *did* want to please God. So I had to let His will preside over my own. To display my true humanity, I will disclose my exact answer.

Ummmmmm I don't really want to... long pause... *but you know I will. If this is what you require of me, I can only ever say YES to you.*

Then, radio silence. I closed my eyes and continued worshiping. Suddenly, an image flashed in my mind: a truck pulling a new camper. It's like I got a glimpse of leaving the old and stepping into the new. Not at all what I expected to see. Was this the plan? Now you see what I was struggling with.

I didn't breathe a word of it to Andrew but only asked God to confirm. Our pastor started preaching a sermon on, get this, "God wants to stretch your yes." What?! I mean come on... not only that, He based the teaching off of the time God asked Abraham to sacrifice Isaac, to give up what God had promised. Well, you don't say. Isn't this what He just asked me to do? I hung on every spirit-filled word and feverishly took notes. He was all up in my mail.

At the end of the sermon, only thirty minutes after God asked me to give up my promise, and I had seen what I wanted to deny, you'll never believe what Andrew leaned over and whispered to me.

"Do you think we are supposed to get a truck and buy our own camper?"

Really God? Well, there was no denying it now. The internal vision and conversation I had with the Holy Spirit, was now being voiced by my husband! I chuckled as I replied, "Yep. That is exactly what we're supposed to do."

I could not believe it. Before this moment of crazy, spot-on confirmation, our whole family was done with camping. But, when I told the kids what God had spoken, they could not wait for us to buy our own Fifth wheel trailer. A complete 180 shift in an instant. A word from the Lord will do that. You know God is in something when the entire family is enthusiastically on board! We didn't even know if we could get a camper, but we all said YES; we'll do it for you, God, and we stepped out in faith and started looking.

We got the confirmation on Sunday, and by Wednesday, we owned a beautiful fifth-wheel camper. The doors flung open. When we were trying to do *our* plan, in our own strength, every single door closed. When we inquired of God for *His* plan for our season,

I'll SAY YES

He answered right away and opened every single door. I've never felt more smack dab in the will of God. It is not what I expected but because I know we were doing exactly what He wanted of us, we had joy and peace.

Sometimes what we think we want, may not be what is best for us for our stage of life. Even though I didn't think I would love camping, maybe God knows what I would like even better than I do. Saying YES might mean fulfilling every dream, but it could also mean surrendering those dreams for a season or forever. But my hope isn't in a dream, it's in my God.

A dream I've been waiting for is the opportunity to use my gift of hospitality. I literally LOVE to have people over. Living in a small space can discourage us from hosting events at our house. I want to put on big dinners with all our friends again and create a community to do life with. Can you relate? Are you waiting on things to change in order for you to pursue a passion?

- When I have the nice house, then I'll host small group.
- When I have the big ministry, then I'll post regular content online.
- When our space is bigger, then I'll have ALL the people over.
- When I have more money, then I'll be generous.
- When I have excess time, then I'll volunteer.

This was one of the hardest things about the nomad season for me, but in the spirit of starting small, we decided to change this. The little boy with his two loaves and fishes didn't have much, but he had something, as all of us do. How often do we respond like the disciples… "but what good is that with this huge crowd?" We perceive we don't have enough (space, time, money, influence) to make a difference, but remember what Jesus did with that little boy's equivalent of a Lunchable?

<u>There's a young boy here with five barley loaves and two fish. But what good is that with this huge crowd?"</u>

"Tell everyone to sit down," Jesus said. So they all sat down on the grassy slopes. (The men alone numbered about 5,000.) <u>Then Jesus took the loaves, gave thanks to God, and distributed them to the people. Afterward he did the same with the fish. And they all ate as much as they wanted.</u>

Jesus thanked God for the small amount He had and when offered for Kingdom use, it was multiplied and blessed MANY. It is time we stop discounting small, little, imperfect, and not a lot. Let's begin thanking God for what we have and asking Him how we can use it. Let's say YES to doing what we can with what we have. I'm not waiting for the farm to host friends, I'm having them over for dinner now. I don't have to wait for a perfect yard to have an outdoor movie night, we are gonna plan a fun summer evening at the camper! It doesn't have to look exactly as we pictured for it to make an impact. Don't wait to live your life until you have a lot. Live to the fullest with whatever you've got and watch all the people God will touch!

> LIVE TO THE FULLEST WITH WHATEVER YOU'VE GOT AND WATCH ALL THE PEOPLE GOD WILL TOUCH!

Saying YES has hidden blessings

So you can bless others while you wait. Are you in a season of a delayed dream? I know how that feels. I believe the temptation in times of waiting is to either want what others have or wonder why they got it before you did. One of the best ways I've discovered to battle discontentment and comparison is to pray for those in the same boat as you.

"Amber, my sister is facing a difficult time. She is living with our parents, working on getting finances figured out, and wants her own home but is not sure how to get it. Would you mind talking with her? I know you can relate," My friend asked me one day during the camper season. Boy, could I relate. Part of me thought, *What do I have to give? I am still here, still clinging for hope; Most days, I want someone to give* me *hope*. But I'm sure I don't need to tell you how I responded.

"YES! Of course, send me her number," I gladly volunteered. I'm always willing to minister, as long as I don't have to rely on my own strength. See, while I may feel empty, God never is. And based on His track record, He has always shown up and worked through me. Jesus always has hope to deal, and if I'll just be a vessel, I'll get to see Him display His glory.

As I spoke with this lovely, but hurting mama, I got to be a listening, unbiased ear. Believe me when I tell you I was praying the entire time for wisdom and for the Holy Spirit to comfort and bring me the right words to be a blessing. We laughed and cheered each other up during our waiting season. When our time together was coming to a close, I knew we had to pray together for her home. Now, she was up against pretty impossible odds, but we recalled that our Father is the God of the impossible, so we asked Him to do just that. Hanging up the phone, I was filled with happiness and so much peace by encouraging another who was in a similar season. Often we think we must be ministered to in order to feel better, but really, we may just need to get our eyes off ourselves, abandon our pity party, and realize it is in blessing others we are built up.

Guess what I heard a few weeks later? "Amber, you are never going to believe this, we got our dream home!" It was not long after we talked that my new friend was about to not only secure the financing but the home of her dreams!!! God did what only He could do, and He got ALL the glory. I celebrated with her as she recounted the whole miraculous story of all the things He lined up for their family. He is so very good.

Have you ever noticed that people around you will get the very thing you are praying for first? I used to think this was pretty messed up until I had an epiphany. We need to flip the script on this lie. God doesn't answer the prayers of others and delay ours because He wants to hurt us. No. He is trying to show us His power, He is showing us: It can be done.

The story of Abraham taught me this. If you are familiar with Abraham's story, you may recall that God promised him a son… but many years later, he still did not have one. His wife's womb was closed up. When traveling through a foreign land, because his wife was so beautiful, Abraham was scared to say Sarah was his wife, for fear the king would kill him and take her for his own. So, he lied and said she was his sister. The king noticed her beauty and brought Sarah into his harem. But God was with Abraham and informed the king, "Oh, I know you did not just take my boy's wife." Okay, that was my version. Next, God comes to the king in a dream, that's where we'll pick up the story…

But that night God came to Abimelech in a dream and told him, "<u>You are</u>

<u>a dead man</u>, *for that woman you have taken is already married!"*

But Abimelech had not slept with her yet, so he said, "Lord, will you destroy an innocent nation? Didn't Abraham tell me, 'She is my sister'? And she herself said, 'Yes, he is my brother.' I acted in complete innocence! My hands are clean."

In the dream God responded, "Yes, I know you are innocent. That's why I kept you from sinning against me, and why I did not let you touch her. Now return the woman to her husband, and he will pray for you, for he is a prophet. Then you will live. But if you don't return her to him, you can be sure that you and all your people will die."

Abimelech got up early the next morning and quickly called all his servants together. When he told them what had happened, his men were terrified. Then Abimelech called for Abraham…

<u>*Then Abraham prayed to God, and God healed Abimelech, his wife, and his female servants, so they could have children. For the LORD had caused all the women to be infertile*</u> *because of what happened with Abraham's wife, Sarah.* Genesis 20:3-8, 17-18, emphasis added

You are a dead man. Haha. God did not mince His words. Now, the king had acted in innocence; It was actually Abraham who had lied and started this whole mess, yet King Abimelech was paying for it. This little fact gives me hope that even though I am not perfect, God will still fight for me. Also, did you notice what God had caused to happen in the king's wife and female servants? They were all infertile until Abraham prayed for them… then, God opened their wombs. Wait, isn't that what Abraham and Sarah were waiting on? Hadn't they been promised a child, but Sarah's womb had not been opened?

The Lord had Abraham pray for the king to receive the exact promise he was believing for! This was no mistake. It was strategic. I believe God wanted to show Abraham He was the God who opens and closes wombs. He is able. Do you know what the very next verse in the Bible is?

The LORD kept his word and did for Sarah exactly what he had promised. She became pregnant, and she gave birth to a son for Abraham in his old age. This happened at just the time God had said it would. Genesis 21:1-2

The very next thing recorded is the promise being fulfilled. This is no coincidence. Abraham had to pray for another to receive what he was waiting for *before* God gave it to him. He had to see it in the life of someone else to revive his hope, not bring discouragement. And so must we. If you are waiting on something for God, look for another who is also waiting and pray with them to receive it. Encourage and bless those whose promise is delayed, and then, when it's fulfilled, rejoice with them! Let it bring you hope!

This YES taught me a few things including trusting God to faithfully guide us on our journey. I learned the value of praying for His plan above my own. When the plan goes off-script, I learned how to actively look for the blessing in my current circumstance. If I took my eyes off God's will, I could quickly spiral into a pit of discouragement by declaring, "This is not what I want!" But what about what He wants? What about His plans for the earth? Where do we fit in? I want to

> **IF YOU ARE WAITING ON SOMETHING FOR GOD, LOOK FOR ANOTHER WHO IS ALSO WAITING AND PRAY WITH THEM TO RECEIVE IT.**

be a part of those plans. This YES showed me how much peace and joy you can find by being smack dab in the middle of the will of God. The contentment found there is unmatched. I learned to start living abundantly now, not when I have more at my disposal. I was also reminded that I am not the only one waiting on a promise, and I can comfort those with the comfort I've received during this camper season.

When you say YES to God, whether life looks like you expected or not, you give Him permission to use your little and multiply it into something bigger than you ever imagined. So I got a few tips I can share from this leg of the journey. First, ask God what His plan is for you right now. Then, embrace the answer. Next, be willing to start living the life you want right now however your circumstance looks. Make the most of it and I guarantee you will chase discontentment away when you see the lives that are impacted by "your little." Last, look for people to encourage who are also waiting. Don't shy away from blessing them because you "haven't arrived." Bless now. Let God minister through you and pray for their promise to come!

Ask God for the plan. Jump onboard. Live life now. Bless and pray for those who are also waiting.

STRETCHING YOUR YES

SCRIPTURE TO APPLY:
And do not forget to do good and to share with others, for with such sacrifices God is pleased. Hebrews 13:16 NIV

SONG TO LISTEN:
"God of Abraham," Vertical Worship

QUESTIONS:
When you witness someone get the miracle you are praying for, how do you react? How has this story challenged your perspective?

Name one thing you have waited to do until circumstances are more ideal. Share about a way you can make it happen now, with what you have.

Ask God "What are you doing in this season?" and write what you sense He replies.

How does this change your perspective? In light of this chapter, what changes are you going to implement in your home and/or life right now?

CHALLENGE:
Consider what you are waiting for. Then, look for someone else who is also waiting for this promise, and commit to pray for and with them.

WILLING VESSELS

Walking with God requires: to be available, live interruptible, and start small. Each time we expand our hearts to allow Him to guide and use us more, we see Him move in ways we never thought possible. God can do anything through anyone. Though man has tried to put Him in a box and say what He does or doesn't do, He will not and cannot be contained. For years, people have wrongly placed other Christians on a pedestal, thinking we could never do what they do. However, it's not the person's power, it is God's. Check out this story:

One day the widow of a member of the group of prophets came to Elisha and cried out, "My husband who served you is dead, and you know how he feared the Lord. But now a creditor has come, threatening to take my two sons as slaves."

"What can I do to help you?" Elisha asked. "Tell me, what do you have in the house?"

"Nothing at all, except a flask of olive oil," she replied.

And Elisha said, "Borrow as many empty jars as you can from your friends and neighbors. Then go into your house with your sons and shut the door behind you. Pour olive oil from your flask into the jars, setting each one aside when it is filled."

So she did as she was told. Her sons kept bringing jars to her, and she filled one after another. Soon every container was full to the brim!

"Bring me another jar," she said to one of her sons.

"There aren't any more!" he told her. And then the olive oil stopped flowing.

When she told the man of God what had happened, he said to her, "Now sell the olive oil and pay your debts, and you and your sons can live on what is left over." 2 Kings 4:1-7

TELL ME WHAT YOU HAVE… this line jumped off the page as I prepared to close out this book with the story of my biggest YES. What do we have to offer a God who needs nothing? Simply ourselves. Our lives. He doesn't need the talented, as we've seen. He doesn't need the rich, our lives made this abundantly clear. He needs a willing vessel. Will you offer your life to Him? Would you climb on the altar of His agenda for the earth and say, "I am a living sacrifice, I will go where you lead, when you lead, and lay down my plans for yours"? Will you say YES and see what He does and where He takes you? I did. And in the next story, I'll tell you where it led.

16

I'll Say Yes
Even if...
I get called crazy

You really gonna make me write this? The tug of my flesh wanted to resist the assignment, but the tug of the Holy Spirit was stronger. I felt more angst over writing this chapter than all the others. This is why it is last. I wanted to say NO to this opportunity because, sometimes when I share it, I am met with resistance. The thought of rejection can keep us from saying YES, can't it? It helps to know Jesus wanted to say no sometimes too, but if He learned to push past His own wishes to honor His Father, then in His strength we can too. We can say "... nevertheless, not my will, but Yours, be done" (Luke 22:42 CSB). So, here goes nothing…

Throughout the pages of this book, I've shared my journey of saying YES to every chance God has given me, but the truth is most of these stories would have never occurred without this YES. This YES had to happen before almost all of the other YES moments I've shared. This YES marked me more than all the others. But, it didn't just mark me, it completely transformed me. My YES journey started with a desire to know the voice of the Holy Spirit, assuming if I said YES every time He spoke, I would hear Him more and He would give me more to do, and it was true and He has. Since I made this deal with God, I was wondering if you and I could make a deal too? How about this: If you start this chapter, you have to finish it! Deal? Okay, cool, you can proceed!

> **THE MOST INCREDIBLY STRETCHING SEASONS OFTEN LEAD TO THE GREATEST GROWTH.**

A few months after I committed to saying YES to God, I encountered the most uncomfortable opportunity of my life, which led to the biggest transformation of my life. Seems about right. The most incredibly stretching seasons often lead to the greatest growth. Here's the story of my biggest YES.

"What the heck is he talking about?" was all I could say. One night, after listening intently to a powerful message, I was puzzled after the minister gave two invitations: one to receive Jesus as Lord and Savior (no questions on this one) and the second for the baptism of the Holy Spirit (lots of questions). I'll never forget Andrew pressing pause on the remote control as we slowly turned to look at each other in confusion. I was twenty-seven and he was twenty-nine, and we had never heard the term in our lives. Now, this is interesting because it's in the Bible, and I had read the entire book, more than once, but we'd never noticed it, and we have attended church since birth. We instantly called our friends who had sent us the sermon with loads of questions.

I've since learned the term "baptism of the Holy Spirit" can cause division. I didn't know this at the time. I'm sharing the exact verbiage the pastor used in his message, but it's also called "being 'filled with the Spirit,'" which is something the disciples both experienced at Pentecost and again later in Acts 4:31, which says:

And when they had prayed, the place where they had gathered together was shaken, and <u>they were all filled with the Holy Spirit and began to speak the word of God with boldness.</u>

What's significant about this passage is these people had *already* been filled with the Holy Spirit once, which assures us believers who have all been given the Holy Spirit at conversion can be filled afresh. They have a fresh boldness. Anyone need that?

Remember the story of the widow and the oil? All she had was oil. When the widow's sons gathered empty vessels, this gave the oil something to fill.

Her sons kept bringing jars to her, and she filled one after another. Soon every container was full to the brim!

Oil represents the Holy Spirit, as we see throughout the Old Testament like when the prophet Samuel anointed David with oil and the Holy Spirit came upon him powerfully. I believe God is looking for willing vessels to pour fresh oil into. Anyone want to be filled to the brim?

Let's jump back to my story, the couple who gave us the sermon to watch walked in more authority and experienced the miraculous like no one I'd ever met! In short, their lives looked like the disciples' did, they had the fruit of the Kingdom and they LOVED Jesus, so I trusted them. They were actually living out the stories of the Bible—regularly seeing miracles of provision and healing, and they taught the Word with authority—if there was something I hadn't been exposed to but they believed it and had scripture to back it, I was willing to listen. Their character and the fruit in their lives gave validity to their words. Pay attention to people's fruit. Are they living how Jesus lived? Are they seeing what He saw? Do they have love, joy, and power or are they condemning, judgemental, and fault-finding?

What our friends did next displayed so much wisdom. They sent us a whole list of Bible verses accompanied with a note, "We'll tell you our story after you read what the Word has to say about this and let God speak to you first." They did not print off a paper of opinions or even share their personal experience; They sent us scripture to look up and research for ourselves. That is exactly what I did. I asked the Holy Spirit to teach me if this was legit or not as one of His roles is to "lead us into all truth." I believe having a teachable heart positions us to see and learn things we never imagined.

I did not immediately write off "the baptism of the Holy Spirit" because some people didn't believe in it. I didn't discount this invitation because I had not heard of it before. I did not assume I "knew it all" on the subject—I certainly did not, and I probably still don't. I did not type it in a search engine or look up what denominational doctrines had to say about it. I did not call other Christians I consider more intelligent than me to get their opinion. I did not ask my pastor or Bible study leader what they thought.

I went to God FIRST, and it made all the difference.

> I WENT TO GOD FIRST, AND IT MADE ALL THE DIFFERENCE.

I went to the One who inspired the phrase and asked Him to explain it to me. I asked Jesus Himself to show me and teach me. And do you know what happened next?! He pulled back an invisible curtain covering my eyes, and I started to see scriptures come alive! I suddenly perceived the Word of God in a new way! Do you know this is something Jesus did for the disciples after He rose from the dead as well? Check this mind-blowing scripture out:

Then he opened their minds so they could understand the Scriptures. Luke 24:45 NIV

There is an unlocking of the mind that can happen, and I experienced it! It's a real thing, guys. Something integral to this story is not letting the word "baptism" trip us up. Do you know what this word means in the original Greek? It simply means "immersion." So *really,* the invitation the pastor gave that night was an invitation to immerse ourselves in the Holy Spirit. He wasn't saying certain believers don't have the Holy Spirit, He was inviting followers of Christ to let the Holy Spirit fully flood *all* of them. Everyone who believes in Christ as their Savior has the same Holy Spirit, Ephesians 1:13 says, 'In him, when you heard the word of truth, the gospel of your salvation, and in him, when you also believed, you were **sealed** with the promised **Holy Spirit**" (ESV, emphasis added). We are all sealed by Him the moment we believe! But does the Holy Spirit have all of us? Have we surrendered every part of our being, our hurts, our full heart, our minds, our bodies to Him? This is a question only you and God can answer.

Up until that point in my life, I had yielded to the Lordship of Jesus as my Savior, but I can honestly say I had not let the Holy Spirit have full reign. I held a lot back. But what really intrigued me in the Word were two scriptures:

"But you will receive <u>power</u> when the Holy Spirit comes on you; and <u>you will</u>

be my witnesses in Jerusalem, and in all Judea, and Samaria, and the ends of the earth." Acts 1:3 NIV, emphasis added

I'm going to shoot straight with you, at the time, I was not walking in any kind of power—but I wanted to. I was not a consistent or bold witness. I knew I was supposed to tell people about Jesus, but I had no passion, never felt equipped, and I was even half scared to have someone overhear me praying or speaking about God in public. I was walking in timidity and lacking confidence. I desired to share about Jesus but also felt nervous and unqualified to do so. Fear and insecurity ran my life, if you can believe it. Here's the other scripture that captivated me as I studied the Holy Spirit:

… how much will the Heavenly Father give the Holy Spirit to those who ask him. Luke 11:13b

Why would Jesus say He would give the Spirit to those who asked? When I entered into a relationship with Jesus, I asked Him to be my Lord, but I did not ask for the Holy Spirit at all. I didn't know I could. We can ask and Jesus says the Father will give? I saw this as a promise. If there was more to experience in the Holy Spirit, this verse proved the Father would allow me to encounter more, if I asked. So guess what I started doing? Asking.

About a week after researching, I knew what I had to do but I wasn't thrilled about it. As I kept digging, I discovered that sometimes when people were filled with the Holy Spirit in the Bible, or refilled, they started speaking in tongues, and this was the most uncomfortable thing I could imagine ever experiencing. I wanted more, but I didn't want that. Haha! It felt out of control and weird.

Growing up, I heard missionaries tell stories of when the gift of tongues was used to help on the mission field, but I never saw it or heard of it in the U.S. Some claim it has ceased. Some say it's done in an unbiblical way, without an interpreter. Some say there is no need for it. But, some say it never stopped. Some believe if it happened in the Bible it can happen today. Some declare if God gave gifts in the scripture, He can and does give these same gifts today. All I know is I wanted to live a life pleasing to God and my one desire was and is to honor Him.

I was so unsure of what would happen if I kept pursuing a life led by and filled with the Holy Spirit. But I wanted more. I wanted to live like the disciples. I wanted the boldness I saw in Peter after he experienced the filling of the Spirit. He stood up, preached a sermon—he never rehearsed, by the way—and thousands of people got saved! I longed to see people healed by the power of Jesus through the obedience of normal people so that they had no other explanation than God is real! *I was done with mundane Christian country club life.* I wanted to walk with God and see the "greater things" Jesus declared we would do in His name that I had yet to see!

I WANTED MORE. I WANTED TO LIVE LIKE THE DISCIPLES.

So one night after popping a bowl of popcorn, I decided it was time to leave my safe, little box, called my friend Holly, and asked if she could come lay hands on me *some time* to be fully immersed in the Holy Spirit. I needed someone to agree with me in prayer. I wanted all of Him and I wanted Him to have all of me. I wanted it ALL. Do you know what she enthusiastically said? "I'll be right over!"

I'LL SAY YES

Nervously I replied, "Like now?"

"Yep! See you in a few minutes!" she said joyfully, hanging up before I had a chance to change my mind. (If this isn't an example of a Spirit-led person, I don't know what is. I'm not sure what Holly was up to that night, but when an opportunity presented itself to be used by God, she dropped everything to go on an unexpected adventure with Him. She allowed God to interrupt her plans. I want to be like this.) I slowly put the phone down and wondered what I had just gotten myself into. I was VERY uncomfortable and, needless to say, I never took one bite of that popcorn; My nerves could not handle it! I wanted to have time to prepare or psych myself up, but I only had minutes before something went down. At first, I thought: *What if nothing happens?* Then, I thought: *What if something does? AWKWARD!!!!!* Either way, awkward!

You still with me? You finishing this chapter? Great, because this is where it gets good! What I am about to tell you is an encounter I may not have believed if it didn't happen to me. Which taught me that just because we haven't experienced something, doesn't mean it can't happen or that it has ceased to exist.

When Holly arrived, we immediately began to pray. Andrew was in the office and when he recounts that night, he says, "As soon as you started praying together it felt like a wind blew through the house."

He experienced one thing, and I experienced another. The moment my friend put her hands on my shoulders, it felt as though I was receiving an electric shock. Something started pulsing through my body. It poured down from the top of my head, and I could feel it flowing to my fingertips and down through my toes.

While the sensation of a supernatural current kept coursing rhythmically through my veins, I was simultaneously praying. In full transparency, I did not know what I was doing or what would happen, but I did know I could trust Him—so I was careful to keep communication open with God. Then it came: A word. One, single word from another language, and first, I heard it in my mind, and then I felt I was also supposed to say it out loud. Since I wasn't quite sure what to do, I prayed internally (and this was integral as the Enemy is not privy to the prayers we have with God in our minds, so he can't counterfeit our confirmation) and asked the Lord, *I am hearing a word, am I supposed to say it? If I am, have Holly say this very word three times in a row.*

Almost as soon as I sent the prayer up to Heaven, I immediately doubted God was going to confirm my request.

Having Holly say a random word from another language three times in a row is like impossible... I then relented my terms, making this outlandish request a little more attainable for God (as if He needed that). True story.

Okay, God, maybe three times is a stretch, how about just having her say it twice?

The *instant* I suggested He lessen the amount, Holly said the *exact* word I was sensing, not one, not two, but guess how many times? THREE! Of course, she did! Are you surprised? And the Holy Spirit followed with:

I'll SAY YES

"You think I can't have her say a specific word three times in a row? Please."

I mean it was instantaneous. And the prayer conversation had been internal. Only God could have heard my prayer and only God could have answered immediately and so specifically.

After laughing at God's statement and having the necessary confirmation, I took a big leap of faith. I spoke this foreign word out loud. Yep, I sure did. Just as YES is only one little word, so uttering this single word was also life-changing. I didn't spout out a steady flow of words but one simple word, and I repeated it over and over. Guys, I am not a crier, but the moment I said it out loud, a dam burst; a hardness was broken that had been preventing a free flow of the Spirit. Tears flooded out of me, and they could not be stopped. I was overwhelmed with wonder and joy.

A YES can completely Change you!

So God really does change a heart from stone to flesh by the power of His Spirit—and I am the proof. The encounter felt like a touch from Heaven and unlike anything I had ever experienced... but as dramatic as it had been, it was not nearly as dramatic as what happened next. I'm referring to the change in me. This is how I know it was God. This is how I know Jesus was in my house that night (it's actually His job to immerse us in the Holy Spirit and Fire). John the Baptist said of Jesus:

John answered all of them: "I baptize you with water, but One more powerful than I will come, the straps of whose sandals I am not worthy to untie. <u>He will baptize you with the Holy Spirit and with fire.</u> Luke 3:16

I was COMPLETELY different the next day, and I have been ever since. It was like the Lord poured His character in and pushed a lot of impurities out. Overnight I went from:

- Judgemental to filled with **compassion**
- Timid and consistently fearful to **bold as a lion**
- Not comfortable sharing my faith to **telling everybody about Jesus**
- Not knowing/understanding scripture to **unpacking** and **speaking verses I had NEVER memorized**
- Not liking a lot of people to **loving everyone**
- Controlling to **letting the Spirit lead**
- Striving for perfection to **going with the flow**

So much deliverance in a moment. I was different in almost every way. I was filled with love, joy, and peace, and I am here to tell you nothing and no one could have done this in my heart except God. You see the list? Look at how I used to be, and then notice the change. Which side looks similar to the attributes of a Pharisee and which looks like Jesus? I'm big enough to admit I had in fact been a very judgemental, religious Christian, but not one filled with the fruit of the Spirit. Chronologically, this moment happened between chapters two and three and looking back, you might notice a shift in my heart towards people. Before, I would hear a command and after a little reluctance I would eventually obey. But after, I not only heard the Holy Spirit, but I actually felt the heart of God for the person which compelled me to be a witness. It was a necessary and needed change to fully walk out my calling. This is when it changed, and this is how it changed.

So that night, Jesus handled His business and dunked me in His Spirit somehow, and all of a sudden, all of the things I used to strive to do in the Bible I was doing with little effort. It was like I had been this ship sailing on the sea getting nowhere, but then, in a moment, my sails went up and the wind of the Holy Spirit blew on me and propelled my faith, witness, and love like never before. The more I prayed in tongues, the more I understood the Bible and the more boldness I had. As I regularly prayed in the Spirit (as Paul calls it in 1 Corinthians 14), His fruit of love, joy, and peace began to manifest exponentially in my life. It was AWESOME! I was on fire, completely fueled by God.

So naturally, I started telling everyone about salvation through faith in Jesus and how the Holy Spirit can empower you to live the Christian life supernaturally. I also disclosed that if you leapt all in with God's Spirit and pursued more, you might just get the gift of tongues too, which is what happened to me. At the time, I didn't quite know how taboo the topic (and all the gifts of the Spirit) was. I just knew what I had experienced.

You know what gave me the courage to write this chapter? The disciples. They had this same encounter, and they didn't hide it. They didn't leave that part out of the Bible because it was different from anything they'd experienced up until that point in their faith journey. No, they wrote it all down and boldly proclaimed what God did for them and through them. And so must I.

What happened next, I did not expect. While I found a lot of people were open to learning more about walking with the Holy Spirit, I encountered some others who did not believe there was any more to experience of God. I began facing MUCH persecution. Oh, it was so very painful. I was new to all of this and I just wanted to share my encounter and lead people to live the victorious Christian life with the Spirit's help, but my message was offensive to some. The reason the persecution hurt me so deeply is like I said, my one desire is to please God in everything I do and say. It's all I ever want to do. But I started being accused of not pleasing God. I couldn't see how. I loved Him more than ever. I shared Jesus more than ever. I could hear Him more than ever. I had the fruit of love, compassion, peace, and joy. It was doctrinal beliefs, opinions, and experiences of man that said it wasn't for now, not the Bible.

During this "trial by fire," I was called about everything you could think of, by Christians. But, I soon discovered what they said about me were the same things people said about Jesus in His day. They say the Devil doesn't have any new tricks, and his plan backfired, because the very words people used to accuse me of not following Jesus, were the very words that confirmed I was. It made me feel better when I discovered in the Word that people who "followed God" and even Jesus' own family said some pretty harsh things about Him, but it didn't hurt any less. Mark 3:21 CEV says, *'When Jesus' family heard what he was doing, they thought he was crazy and went to get him under control."* And look at this passage from Matthew 12:24:

But when the Pharisees heard about the miracle, they said, "No wonder he can cast out demons. He gets his power from Satan, the prince of demons."

Y'all, they literally called God in the flesh demonic, crazy, out of control, and said He got His power from Satan. WHAT?! But this passage from John 15:20 comforted me: "A servant is not greater than his master. If they persecuted me, they will persecute you also." So, if they're saying the same things about you that they said about Jesus, you may actually be following in His footsteps.

I'LL SAY YES

Do you know, up until this time in my faith journey, I had never been persecuted like this, by anyone? Well, isn't that interesting? Since I was being labeled with the same names they called Jesus—I felt I was in good company. I had to learn to be around people who thought I was crazy and unbiblical. This was the journey God took me on to cut off the need for approval from people. I had to live by His opinion because I sure couldn't live by the opinions of others... This is a difficult journey, the narrow path to life, and one God leads His people through. Losing the approval of people to gain and live by the approval of God alone is a needed lesson. He takes all his kids down this road, just look at Mary.

She got pregnant, outside of marriage, with God's baby. Ummmm, what do you think the people in her village said about her? Said to her? Y'all, God ONLY revealed to Joseph and her cousin Elizabeth the baby was from Him... no one else got this message. You better believe Mary was talked about her whole life. There was no way anybody but Joe and cousin 'Liz believed she was walking with God. As a matter of fact, they probably thought she was as far from God as you can get. Crazy. Unbiblical. Not honoring God. And so, Mary had to learn to live by what God said and nobody else. She had to learn to shake off the opinions of others and embrace the opinion of God because what was in her was indeed of the Holy Spirit, even if almost no one else thought so. It wasn't and isn't an easy journey, but it is a necessary one.

So now you see why I opened this chapter the way I did. I love what happened *in* me, but I didn't love the persecution that happened *to* me because of this YES. When God put it on my heart to go public with this part of my journey, I had a choice to make. As I was deciding, a movie hit the theaters: *Top Gun Maverick*. It broke all kinds of records, and while it made a huge splash on the big screen, there was one conversation that reminded me the risk is worth it. Maverick is asked to train young pilots for a potential suicide mission. It's risky and possibly lethal. His friend, and fellow officer, Hondo helps Mav process his decision:

"It's not too late to stop, buddy. You know what happens to you if you go through with this."

"I know what happens to everyone else if I don't."[5] Maverick replies.

Wow. This was a timely word for me. I know what sharing my story has sometimes led to in the past, but I also know that what God did in me He can do in others. I had to be willing to lay my reputation on the altar again for the sake of those who might be forever changed by this YES.

A YES can bring Revival!

So the Holy Spirit is the key element in experiencing revival. Honestly, the verbiage of filling of the Spirit and the gifts of the Spirit is a source of division in the body of Christ and another reason I hesitated to tell my story. I NEVER want to divide and my passion is to bring UNITY to His body… I think the Enemy has divided believers over this long enough. With the world the way it is, we need all of God we can get! We need all the power. All the love. All the wisdom. All the boldness.

If God is the same yesterday, today, and forever… Why can't what happened in the Bible still happen today? If the disciples spoke in tongues, how can it be considered unbiblical or ungodly? I do believe the Devil loves to pervert the gifts of God, and some have spoken of and used the Holy Spirit's gifts inaccurately. I believe there are cults who have attempted to mimic and try to invalidate the various gifts. The Enemy has attacked this area relentlessly—but we have got to ask ourselves: WHY? Why would he not want us to get immersed deeper into the Holy Spirit or have any of the Spirit's gifts manifest?

He's scared, that's why. The Devil knows if God's people are soaked in God's Spirit—walking in not only the power and authority of Christ but possessing the character of Jesus—His day is DONE.

We must always be discerning. The Bible says if it is truly the Holy Spirit, then He will glorify Jesus, not some other prophet, teacher, or leader (He will glorify Me, for He will take from that which is Mine and will disclose it to you. John 16:14 BSB). The focus will always be Jesus, His finished work of the cross, and the love of the Father. He heals because He loves, He gives a Word of knowledge because He wants to draw people to Himself. Everything points back to and glorifies God, not another human. We must always hold teachings and demonstrations up to scripture. Is it being done in the Biblically instructed way? Is the Kingdom of God being furthered? Are the fruit of the Spirit present?

Although my journey with being immersed in the Holy Spirit began with some resistance, God led our family to an incredible church home here in the Carolinas. Our pastors and leaders not only teach Christians how to be filled with the Spirit but embrace and empower us to operate in all the gifts of the Holy Spirit and the gifts Christ gave the church. Everything is backed by the Bible, and we are seeing the fire of God touch our community through ordinary people. Revival is stirring—Jesus is exalted, the gospel is preached, people are being led by the Spirit, and we are seeing literal miracles. It's exciting as our Christian walk should be!

If you are interested in learning more about this, pray and ask the Holy Spirit to teach you, flip over to page 228 and read through the scriptures, and be teachable and open to whatever God wants to reveal to you. This was my YES to the Holy Spirit, but you gotta have your own. He is your friend and teacher. He may take you somewhere unexpected and possibly uncomfortable, but I can promise you will see and experience the power of God, the "greater things" Jesus said we would see and do (John 14:12).

That's the story of my personal revival. If you want to be on fire for God, get to know the Holy Spirit. If you want to know more about Jesus, ask the Spirit to teach you. If you want to connect with God as Father, that's the Spirit's job. It turns out, He is not only supposed to be our best friend but the one who:

- Helps us (John 4:16)
- Transforms us into the likeness of Christ (2 Corinthians 8:18)
- Is the key to our freedom (2 Cor 3:17)
- Unveils and glorifies Jesus(John 16:14).
- Reveals God as our Father, (Romans 8:15)
- Changes our heart of stone into flesh (Ezekiel 36:26)

We cannot and will not go deeper without Him. We need Him for ALL of it. Getting closer to God is *only* done through the work of the Holy Spirit.

As is evident by my many stories and especially this heart-transforming one, while saying YES to God can be incredibly nerve-wracking for a moment, the results can literally change your life and the life of many others. But saying YES doesn't always come without a cost. When I said YES to going deeper, I faced the worst persecution of my life, by the religious community, no less… but consequently, this is the exact group who persecuted Jesus. They believed in God, but they also thought they "knew it all" when it came to the things of the Lord. But all their knowledge left them puffed up, leaving them blinded by pride to see God in the flesh walking right in front of them. I don't want to miss God, and I sense that neither do you.

> IF YOU WANT TO BE ON FIRE FOR GOD, GET TO KNOW THE HOLY SPIRIT.

When we say YES to God, we'll never regret it. We may look crazy to others, but it's only because we're crazy about Jesus! By saying YES, we learn many necessary lessons. A few tips this HUGE YES taught me was first, *really living* means letting the Spirit lead. So do that. Let the Holy Spirit of God be your guide, in everything. Let the Word of God confirm His will, not the opinions of man. Secondly, be open to whatever God wants to do, whatever it looks like. He cannot and will not be boxed. God is God and He can do what He wants. Allow Him to break down any walls and beliefs you've had of Him, the Holy Spirit, and the gifts of the Spirit, and let Jesus do whatever He wants to in your life. Third, you must learn to live by the opinion of God alone, and you will *truly* be free, not held back by others but empowered by God Himself to boldly tell others about Jesus and the salvation available to them! Fourth, you are allowed to ask for more! You are allowed to ask God to fill you and refill you! We are leaky vessels, and when we pour out, we need to be filled back up.

Let the Spirit lead. Be open to God. Live by His opinion. Ask for more!

STRETCHING YOUR YES

SCRIPTURE TO APPLY:
And now I will send the Holy Spirit, just as my Father promised. But stay here in the city until the Holy Spirit comes and fills you with power from heaven. Luke 24:49

SONG TO LISTEN:
"Rest on Us," Maverick City Music & UPPERROOM
"Make Room," The Church Will Sing, Elyssa Smith

QUESTIONS:
How did this chapter challenge you?

Have you surrendered all of yourself to the Holy Spirit? Have you said, "Fill every part of me, I am not holding anything back"? Why or why not?

Are there aspects of the Holy Spirit or the gifts of the Spirit that make you uncomfortable? What are they? Why?

Share about a time you sensed or heard the Holy Spirit.

Do you want more of His power active in your life?

CHALLENGE:
Ask God for more. Be willing to let Him examine you and reveal any areas you have not yielded to His Spirit. Ask Jesus to immerse you in the Spirit of God afresh and to set you on fire for His Kingdom.

Conclusion

To wrap it all up: Say yes to God. Need I say more? It's pretty much the best advice I can give you. It's not fancy or eloquent, but it is potent and life-altering. You will never regret following Him! You won't get to the end of your life and wonder "What would have happened if I had said YES?" You will know because you gave your YES to God, every time.

I shared many of my tips with you but giving God your YES will teach you custom-made life lessons. I hope you are inspired to lay your life down on the altar and make yourself a living sacrifice, ever available to Jesus. When your availability intersects with His ability, you see His power at work. When you choose to allow your schedule to be interrupted for His greater plan, you get to see miracles. When you sow your "little" into the Kingdom of God, you get to witness His multiplication. When you allow yourself to be a vessel of His love, He will change you and change others around you. When you say YES and trust God with the rest, you will see the glory of God.

So the question is, the next time the Holy Spirit asks you to do something, what will you say? I hope you answer:

> I'll Say Yes!

YOUR YES STORY!

You've read my stories, now I want to read yours! When have you said YES to God and seen Him move in power? Maybe this is new for you and you haven't witnessed Jesus show up in an impactful way. I promise as you say YES, you will. When that happens, send me your story. I can't wait to read about you stepping out of your comfort zone to respond to the call of God! And, if you'll allow me, I'd like to share your story! I'll be posting snippets of all the stories I receive on my Instagram pages: @amberolafsson and our ministry page @unitedhouseministries

Let's see what God can do with a bunch of people who say YES!

Email your YES stories to: illsayyesbook@gmail.com

Were you encouraged by this book? Please let others know by sharing about it online! When you leave reviews on Amazon, it helps tell other people about this message. The more people saying YES to God, the more revival we will see! I value every post, share, and review!

SAY YES TO A RELATIONSHIP WITH JESUS

You may have read this whole book and wondered, "Am I even saved?", "Do I have a relationship with God", or "How do I start walking with the Lord?" Well if that's you, I have the solution:

Ask Jesus to be the Lord of your life. It's really simple to start a relationship with God. Just ask Him to be a part of your life, declare with your mouth that you are making Jesus your Lord, and believe that after He died on the cross, rose from the dead, and lives forever in Heaven interceding on your behalf. Jesus paid for every sin we would ever commit on the cross, and when He died, that sin went into the grave. When He arose, He left your sin and my sin there, never to be put on our record again. When He ascended to heaven, He made us right with God! He died for our sin, but He rose for our righteousness.

It's a pretty sweet deal, you go from trusting your works to trusting in Jesus' work. Every person gets to decide if they want to have faith in themself, faith in "I am good enough to get to God," or they can have faith in Jesus, faith in "Jesus was good enough to restore my relationship with God." Where do you place your faith? In your works? Your obedience? Or in Jesus' work? Jesus' obedience? My faith is in Jesus, I am not and cannot be my own Savior, no one can. Either we are perfect or we need a Savior! We need someone to pay the price and bridge the gap between us and God. Jesus did. By putting your faith in Jesus, you become right with God.

The Bible says:

If you openly declare that Jesus is Lord and believe in your heart that God raised him from the dead, you will be saved. For it is by believing in your heart that you are made right with God, and it is by openly declaring your faith that you are saved. Romans 10:9-10

Prayer:

Dear Jesus, I want to start a relationship with you today! I am not putting faith in myself, my good works, or my obedience anymore! I am putting my faith in you! Please forgive me of all my sins and wash me as pure as snow. I want to live the rest of my life with you! From today on, I will follow you! In Jesus' name, I pray, Amen!

Welcome to the family!!

If you made this decision, please let me know! Email me at illsayyesbook@gmail.com and I will send you a free gift!

Say Yes to the Holy Spirit

The second you asked Jesus to be your Lord and Savior, you were sealed with the Holy Spirit… but now I ask you, do you want Him to empower you for ministry? Do you want to see Him move more powerfully in your life? Do you want Him to give you more boldness, pour in God's love, and set your heart on fire?! He can and He will. Ask God to teach you more about the Holy Spirit. Take time to read all of these scriptures and ask the Holy Spirit to teach you about Himself. Get to know Him. Write down what He reveals.

Matthew 3:11
John 20:21-22
Ephesians 1:13-17
Luke 24:49
Acts 1:4, 8
Acts 2: 1-4
Acts 11:14-18
Acts 4:31
Acts 11: 15-16
1 Corinthians 14: 18, 4, 2, 28, 15-17
Acts 10:44-47
Acts 8: 14-17
Acts 19: 2-6

Mark 16:17
Romans 8:26
Jude 20

Prayer:

Dear God, I want more of you. I want to see You move in my life as You did with the disciples. I pray for your Holy Spirit to fill all of me. If I have held anything back from you, I release it now. Have your way. Immerse me in your Holy Spirit and fire. In Jesus' name, I pray, Amen!

ACKNOWLEDGEMENTS

To God the Father, Son, and Holy Spirit: Thank you for using someone like me! Thank you for asking me on this adventure! Thank you for speaking to and leading me! I love being your hands and feet in this world! I pray that after people read this book You have a whole lot more people saying YES to Your God-opportunities!

To my family, Andrew, Drew, Emma, and Jack (aka the Dream Team): Thank you for helping me live every page of this book. You were with me each time I said YES to God whether in support or actively involved. My adventures always involve our family and you guys are all in! Let's keep saying YES and see where the Holy Spirit takes us next!

To my parents, Tim and Sheryl, Thor and Glenida: Thank you for believing in and constantly praying for me! Thank you for supporting our ministry, music, many entrepreneurial ventures, and modeling to us Christian businesses ownership! We would not be where we are and this book would not even exist if it wasn't for you!

To Jessica, my friend, General Manager, and constant support/cohort with all my many schemes and dreams: Thank you for the hours upon hours of phone calls, late-night texts, planning, executing, and tireless work on this book AND on some of these YESes! Where would I be without you? You keep me grounded but also are into the details! Grateful for you!

To the United House Publishing team: Thank you for making me look smarter and more creative than I actually am! I'm grateful for every suggestion, each prayer, and all of the time you invested into this book and our company. I just love being in the "making dreams come true" business with you. This company was born from a YES to God, but each day, you say YES to helping others get their message out! You matter! Your work matters!

To Kristy, Angela, and Stacey: Thank you for praying me through this writing and publishing season! Thank you for joining me on some of these YES adventures! I'm SO grateful to have friends who also say YES to God and inspire me! Your examples of faithfulness to go wherever and whenever God calls encourages me DAILY.

To Melissa: Thank you for telling me, "I can't wait to read your book about saying YES to God, full of all your stories." I can't count how many times you said that! I promise you, this book would not be in your hands had you not spoken that over and over. I wrote this for you, ya know! Here it is! Your encouragement got me to the finish line!

To my Woman Arise Sisterhood: Thank you for encouraging me to focus on and finish this book now! Thank you for declaring this to be a year of supernatural acceleration and boy was it ever! Natalie, you made me set that goal of writing a few chapters, and then, low and behold, within months it was complete, quite by surprise! Rach, you reminded me to "sit my butt in the chair and write" when I wanted to work on all the other things! You prayed over me and guided me, and I needed it, guys! Sarah—you encouraged me every time I posted, when I thought I wasn't making a difference, you were my "one." I posted for you! Emma—you said I was kind and how much you loved me; I needed to hear that! Heidi—girl you make me laugh but the way God has knit us together over our plants and kids and lives has been the blessing I've needed. Melissa—your revelations and calling out of my Kingdom identity have breathed destiny over me! Jalaiyah—your soothing voice and determination to not let me speak negatively reminded me that God can use my voice. I'm grateful!!

To my IMPACT gals: Thank you for your constant support and prayers! Our conversations and calls have been the source of joy and inspiration in writing! You are one of my YESes. Every note, prayer, comment, and text have come precisely when I needed it!

To Jason and Nicole: Thank you for seeing potential in me and calling it out! You'll never know how your investment changed and challenged me. I am forever grateful for your leadership, and what you taught me has impacted everything I've done since. You are leaders of leaders! Truly. Your impact is way more than you can fathom! Thank you!

To The Light Conference women: Thank you for coming from far and wide to meet with God. Because you said YES to attending, we get to see miracles and lives changed together! Let's keep shining our light ladies!

To Christine: Thank you for letting a normal girl who just loves Jesus be your camp pastor! It is the highlight of my summer and seeing Jesus touch the kids every year is life-changing. Thank you for saying YES to your God dream! I couldn't have picked a more perfect person to get the property after my family! You are using it all for the Kingdom! You are changing lives!

To Multiply church: Thank you for covering us and our ministry! Thank you for calling out the evangelist and apostle gifting in Andrew and me. Thank you for listening to the Holy Spirit with every message you preach and every experience you lead! We are grateful for a church home that invites the presence of God and stirs the coals of revival every week. We are blessed to be here!

To everyone who has helped with United House Ministries: Thank you for saying YES to volunteering! Because of your faithfulness, we have seen God do absolute miracles! We could not have led Freedom Nights, The Light Conference, or launched United House Worship without you! We love you and are grateful for you!

To Holly: Thank you for dropping everything and coming over that night eleven years ago—for saying "YES God, I'll go now!" That moment marked me forever, and I hope it leads to many more lives being changed for the glory of God. He has seen your faithfulness! He is multiplying it!

To Phyllis: Thank you for every single word of encouragement! I know I didn't share a story about you in this book, but your prayers and uplifting words have inspired me to write it all down. You truly believe in me and that it's rare to have such an extravagant supporter! Thank you for your YES, for listening to the promptings of God to support and lift me up! I'm grateful, I wanted you to know I'm grateful!

Bibliography

1. Vawser, Lana. "Happily Interruptible." Instagram, June 19, 2022. https://www.instagram.com/p/Ce-kLCcug9-/?igshid=YmMyMTA2M2Y.

2. Eldredge, John, and Stasi Eldredge, *Captivating: Unveiling the Mystery of a Woman's Soul*. Nashville: Thomas Nelson, 2021.

3. Osteen, Joel. "Being Content Right Where You Are." Instagram. Accessed August 4, 2022. https://www.instagram.com/tv/CUAVjfztXtf/?igshid=YmMyMTA2M2Y.

4. MovieQuotesandMore.com. "Top Gun: Maverick (2022) Best Movie Quotes." MovieQuotesandMore. Accessed August 15, 2022. https://www.moviequotesandmore.com/top-gun-maverick-new-quotes/.

About the Author

Amber is first and foremost a daughter of the Most High and lover of Jesus. She wears many hats including wife, mom, author, Kingdom entrepreneur, ministry leader, and good news spreader. Amber has a passion to see people encounter God and watch their lives be set ablaze with His holy fire.

She and her husband co-founded United House Ministries and United House Worship. Together, they own Allegiance Coffee, a craft coffee shop company that employs and empowers individuals with disabilities and creates opportunities for people to own their own businesses. Amber is also the owner of the Christian publication company United House Publishing and founder of The Light Conference.

The Olafssons live with their three energetic, world-changing kiddos, and her ever-growing flock of chickens and livestock guardian dog Lila, in North Carolina. When she is not relaxing on the back patio with a good book and a hot cup of coffee, she enjoys writing, helping others tell their stories, taking trips with her family, and spending time at the feet of Jesus. Check out her other books: *THE AWESOME ONE*, *Dynamite Love*, and *Capture Your Audience* online, and to learn more about her day-to-day life follow her on Instagram @amberolafsson